ON NEGOTIATING
WITH CUBA

Roger W. Fontaine

American Enterprise Institute for Public Policy Research
Washington, D. C.

Roger W. Fontaine is director of Latin American Studies at the Center for Strategic and International Studies at Georgetown University.

ISBN 0-8447-3191-9

Foreign Affairs Study 28, December 1975

Library of Congress Catalog Card No. 75-39898

© 1975 by American Enterprise Institute for Public Policy Research, Washington, D. C. Permission to quote from or to reproduce materials in this publicaton is granted when due acknowledgment is made.

Printed in the United States of America

ON NEGOTIATING
WITH CUBA

CONTENTS

1
INTRODUCTION

The United States seems to be, in the words of Dean Acheson, "approaching the end of an error" in its policy toward Cuba. After several false starts, the Organization of American States sanctions against Cuba were virtually abandoned by the OAS foreign ministers at the San José, Costa Rica, meeting held in July 1975. Moreover, American officials now talk openly of negotiating with the Cuban government in the near future. Despite the growing demand for a change in policy, however, little analysis of what is involved in resuming relations with Cuba has been attempted. The expectation seems to be that a revision of American policy is urgently needed and the rest will somehow fall into place. Taking no thought for the morrow may be good Christianity, but it is not prudent statecraft.

This essay's central assumption is that, while relations with Cuba are inevitable (though not necessarily desirable), the precise nature of these relations is still very much open to question. For example, will it be easier for the United States to deal with Fidel Castro, the pro-Soviet Communist of 1975, than it was to handle the Jacobin nationalist of 1959? Are we faced with the prospect of a permanent Soviet military base in the Caribbean or is that worry irrelevant in an era of détente and long-range nuclear weapons? Assuming that the Cubans have dropped their strategy of promoting guerrilla warfare, does that signal a rapprochement with the United States or merely the substitution of some more effective anti-American policy?

American leaders have more than these issues to worry about. They must also be aware of the long history, often unhappy and often distorted for partisan advantage, of Cuban-American relations. They must also face the fact that our dealings with Cuba have been and will always be a classic instance of a big power-little power confrontation. And last, they must come to terms with the mistakes and false perceptions that have dogged American policy in the recent past.

Once past errors are understood, there is the problem of fashioning a workable strategy for the coming negotiations. First, American leaders must come to grips with Cuban and Soviet ambitions in the region—both their objectives and their strategy—before sorting out American goals in the future talks. Nothing could be more foolhardy than a fatuous optimism over these negotiations, an optimism based on the notion that bad relations were and are simply the result of U.S. intransigence. Finally, we must ask what specific issues need to be discussed and what can we reasonably expect from these discussions?

Cuban-American relations, past, present, and probably future, are not an easy or pleasant subject to examine. At every turn we encounter failures, mistakes, cross-purposes, and great, perhaps unbridgeable, differences. Yet we remain near neighbors, as the Cuban premier has recently reminded us, and some kind of modus vivendi will be worked out. This essay is an attempt to discuss the problems of doing so and to lay out the best strategy for the coming negotiations. There is no perfect solution, and none is offered here, but it is at least possible to expose some of the hidden rocks on which previous American leaders have seen their policies wrecked.

2
CUBA AND THE UNITED STATES: FROM THE BEGINNINGS TO 1959

Let us begin with the obvious. The current sorry state of Cuban-American relations is in part the result of problems that have continually plagued Cubans in the course of the island's history—and that have intermittently concerned, and baffled, Americans. But what happened before 1959 did not determine the course of the Cuban revolution. The current regime is certainly not inexplicable in terms of the Cuban past—but Fidel Castro was not inevitable nor did the United States necessarily deserve what it got.

But while historical inquiry can indicate the problem areas of Cuban-American relations, there is no agreement on precisely what the problems are and exactly who is to blame. In fact, there are three contending interpretations of the history of Cuban-American relations.

The first, basically Marxist, and of course favored in Havana, assumes that the United States is the villain. Its greed for empire and treasure drove it to preventing an authentically Cuban regime from taking power—at least until 1959. After that, quite naturally, it made every attempt to destroy the new regime.

The second interpretation comes close to the *Cuba sí, Yanqui sí* model: mistakes have been made on both sides, though the United States is perhaps the worse offender; with a measure of understanding and patience, however, even the United States's hostility can be resolved eventually. After all, if the United States can work with the Soviet leaders and the Chinese, surely the neighboring Cubans can also be caught in the net of détente.[1]

---

[1] It is often overlooked that the China-U.S.S.R. analogy is, for a number of reasons, not very appropriate for Cuba. That small Communist state is much closer in outlook and self-interest to North Vietnam and North Korea which have also resisted ending the cold war.

The third position assumes that mistakes have been made by the United States and Cuba, both before and after 1959, but emphasizes fundamental differences rooted in conflicting interests, passions, and perceptions of one another that will never be resolved easily or completely. Cuban-American relations will continue to be difficult at best, if not virtually impossible.

But whichever of these interpretations one accepts, neither the Castro government nor American dealings with it will ever be comprehensible unless the past is weighed and found wanting, in terms of both what the Cubans have done to themselves and what we have done to and for them. Therefore, this study will attempt, first, a sketch of the island's political history; second, an examination of the quality of Cuban nationalism; and third, an analysis of the course of Cuban-American relations. In fact, the more one looks at the latter, the clearer it becomes that present difficulties are far from novel. It is also apparent (though rarely stated) that within a larger context these two countries have no choice but to embark on one of the most difficult ventures in international relations: diplomacy between the grossly unequal.

Cuba's Past

A capsule version of Cuban history will serve our purpose here.[2] Cuba, discovered by Columbus during his first voyage in quest of India, remained under Spanish control for four centuries. Cuba and Puerto Rico were the last remnants of the Spanish empire in the Western Hemisphere, only freed from Spanish domination in 1898. Even so, the sobriquet "ever-faithful isle"—bestowed by a Bourbon monarch for Cuba's refusal to recognize a Bonaparte claimant to the Spanish throne—is misleading.

In fact, Cuban history is filled with rebellion, which, over the centuries, involved nearly all the colony's social classes. The most important revolts included a slave uprising in 1533, creole rebellions in 1721 and 1723, and the formation of revolutionary secret societies in 1823. In the 1850s Cuban exile groups based in the United States unsuccessfully attempted landings on the island. In 1868 a guerrilla war broke out in the eastern provinces. It lasted ten years and left Cuba prostrate—and still under Spanish control. Yet another rebellion broke out in 1895. For three years the new conflict resembled

---

[2] The best accounts of Cuban history in English are Hugh Thomas, *Cuba: The Pursuit of Freedom* (New York: Harper and Row, 1971), and Willis F. Johnson, *The History of Cuba* (New York: B. F. Buck, 1920), 5 volumes.

the earlier inconclusive struggle, until the United States entered the fight by declaring war on Spain on 25 April 1898.

The Spanish were defeated in short order, but Cuba remained under foreign control with an American military governor until May 1902. For the next twenty years, the new Cuban republic was torn apart by periodic civil wars conducted by factions disguised as political parties. To add to Cuban difficulties, the United States felt compelled to intervene on two occasions (1909 and 1917), though it avoided involvement in a bloody race war that broke out in 1912. In 1925 General Gerardo Machado, succeeding to the presidency by both the ballot and the bullet, promised reform and order. Instead he established a dictatorship that lasted until August 1933 when, after two years of urban terror capped by a general strike and American withdrawal of support, Machado was driven into exile.

After a short-lived provisional government led by Grau San Martín, who promised extensive reforms, the Cuban army, freshly purged of its officer corps, came to power under the command of ex-sergeant Fulgencio Batista. For six years, Batista remained the *éminence grise* of the regime, but in 1940 he was elected president under a new constitution. Four years later he surrendered the office to a political opponent, Grau San Martín, the man he had removed from power in 1933. Again in 1948, elections were held and Grau's labor minister, Prío Socorrás, succeeded to the presidency. The twelve years from 1940 to 1952 were the extent of Cuba's experiment with liberal democracy, and they were tarnished with violence, corruption and, above all, a sense of malaise and disappointment. It is not surprising, then, that when Batista returned to the presidential palace with the help of the army, he was virtually unopposed.

Cuban passivity, however, proved only temporary; Batista could no more enjoy his tyranny than Machado had before him. By 1956 he was faced with urban insurrection followed by guerrilla warfare led by Fidel Castro, who by that time had a decade of violent political action behind him. Batista's stay in office lasted less than six years. When Cubans woke up on New Year's Day 1959, they found themselves without a tyrant and with a hope that their country would finally break from its past of violence, corruption, and foreign intervention to become prosperous, stable, and democratic. This was another hope that would be disappointed. But were politically aware Cubans asking too much? To answer that question, two other aspects of Cuban history need deeper probing.

The Character of Spanish Colonialism. Unlike British rule in America, Spanish colonialism had almost no redeeming features whatsoever. The Spaniards neglected Cuba in favor first of Hispaniola (present-day Santo Domingo and Haiti) and then of Mexico. Consequently Cuba was never administered by the best men. In fact, by the mid-sixteenth century the colony had fallen into decline as settlers moved on, either in the expectation of greater opportunities elsewhere in the Spanish new world or in fear of French pirates.[3] But despite Spain's inability to fulfill the most elementary functions of government, it did lay claim to absolute authority over the colony.

Cuba was ruled, in theory, like any home province, though without the privileges some of them had managed to retain. But centralized authority did not amount to centralized rule. The distance between Madrid and Havana made that quite impossible. Rule was both arbitrary and haphazard. No wonder, then, that laws created far away and often unsuited to local conditions went unenforced. This situation soon bred a disrespect for authority that made later attempts at balancing authority with liberty all but futile. Moreover, non-rule from Madrid—not benign neglect in Cuba's case, but malign impotence—did not gradually foster a demand for orderly self-rule in Cuba.

Instead, Spain's appointed governors acted in their own self-interest, which meant growing as rich as possible as soon as possible.[4] The Spanish crown, naturally, was aware of the abuse and attempted to curb corruption by permitting its representatives only short terms in office.[5] This measure, however, only stimulated their rapaciousness and made it impossible for the occasional able and honest man to deal intelligently with the colony's problems.

Cubans may not have whittled away Spanish authority by insisting on governing themselves, but they were hardly docile. As noted above, rebellions were frequent and bloody. The causes of their failure were many, but two are of particular interest. First, the great revolts of the nineteenth century occurred after Spain had lost most of its empire, so the metropole was able to devote a large part of its

---

[3] The French attacked and occupied Santiago in July 1533, and proceeded to do the same to Havana in the following year. Johnson, *History of Cuba*, volume 1, pp. 166, 184-88.

[4] The greed of one governor, Lieutenant General Leopoldo O'Donnell y Jovis (1843-1848), was legendary. Not only did he impose his own personal tax, but he had his wife supervise Havana's orphans in the making of bedding which they later sold in Spain. Hudson Strode, *The Pageant of Cuba* (New York: John Day Co., 1936), pp. 82-83.

[5] From 1762 to 1898, Spain appointed seventy-three governors which meant an average term of office of less than two years. Thomas, *Cuba*, Appendix II, pp. 1,508-10.

military strength to holding down the "ever-faithful isle."[6] The second and probably more important explanation of their failure was the lack of unity among the Cuban people. The root of their disunity was fear of what might happen once independence was achieved—namely, a great slave revolt—a fear that the Spanish authorities were only too happy to encourage.

It was not wholly unfounded. Through much of the nineteenth century, the white populations of the Caribbean as well as of the southern United States remembered the great Haitian slave uprising of the 1790s. No one, of course, wanted a second Haiti, but no one was sure how to prevent it, and it seemed to many that a quick end to Spanish authority could bring it on. Cuba had already experienced slave revolts, and the fact that they had been suppressed did not make white creoles sleep any easier at night.

Cuba, then, had the misfortune of having to confront two great issues at the same time: slavery and independence. Unlike the United States, it never had the opportunity to deal with them separately. With its sugar-based economy, Cuba was entirely a slave society and its patriots had to face the consequences of that fact.[7] Moreover, separation from Spain was not a widely shared goal. Middle-class support was entirely lacking in the nineteenth century. The urban middle class especially, dominated by Spanish merchants who were more royalist than the king, not only did not favor independence, but actively opposed it. After the Ten Years' War broke out in October 1868,[8] these Havana merchants, unaided, raised a volunteer army of 30,000 within three months to fight the rebels.

The war itself deserves further examination. This great tragedy of Cuba's long colonial history is seen by the Castro regime as the genesis of its revolutionary tradition. That is to say, the present Cuban leaders have used the great insurrection to legitimize their own. But their interpretation neatly evades the terrible legacy of that war. We have seen that the Cubans faced the problem of achieving independence and dealing with slavery all at the same time. This difficulty was reflected in the so-called *"grito de Yara"* issued by

---

[6] In the second year of the Ten Years' War (1869), the Spanish army numbered 40,000 soldiers. Ibid., p. 244.

[7] Until the 1850s at least, Cuban creole hopes for independence from Spain were linked with schemes of annexation to the United States. Indeed, the desire to separate from Spain may well have been stimulated by Spanish talk of emancipation which in part was a result of British abolitionist pressure. C. Stanley Urban, "The Africanization of Cuba Scare, 1853-1855," *Hispanic-American Historical Review*, vol. 37 (1957), pp. 29-45.

[8] Manuel de Céspedes, the liberal planter who led the revolt, checked the Spanish threat to emancipate by freeing his own slaves. Thomas, *Cuba*, pp. 245-46.

Manuel de Céspedes, an Oriente landowner and leader of the revolt, who called for revolution based on the proposition that all men are created equal, but insisted that slaves would have to be satisfied with gradual emancipation.

The disaster of Cuba's first great war of independence can be appreciated better (though hardly definitively) by comparison with the American one. In the first place, the American Revolution lasted not ten but seven years and, moreover, ended in success. Also, the American war was much closer to a conventional military campaign; Cuba's was guerrilla warfare at its most brutal. The cost in lives was over a quarter of a million and property damage (which was the principal military objective of the insurgents) has been figured at $300 million.[9] The brutality shown by both sides made compromise impossible and had a corrupting effect on the revolutionaries themselves. Céspedes, the gentleman planter, was soon replaced by men of less scruples. No wonder, then, that one British historian should characterize the revolution as "less a war than a breakdown of order."[10] He adds:

> To a great extent the war consisted of a formalization of the violent banditry that had gone on through much of the early nineteenth century; escaped slaves now proclaimed themselves rebels and in place of *rancheadores* sent by the Conde de Casa Barreto, the Spanish army and its allies (themselves half-bandits) pursued them half-heartedly while regaling themselves with rum at the Spanish government's cost.[11]

This decade of violence was fruitless. Later interpretations notwithstanding, the Ten Years' War did not bring about the political founding of the Cuban nation. Again in contrast to their American counterparts who created the Continental Congress, the rebels did not establish a workable political body. Neither the Cuban exile junta nor the rebel house of representatives could be considered such.[12] What effective political organization did exist lay within the

---

9 Strode, *Pageant of Cuba*, p. 109.
10 Thomas, *Cuba*, p. 254. The men who replaced Céspedes, Maximo Gómez and especially Antonio Maceo, though heroes to Cubans of all political persuasions, were as ruthless as the Spanish, and neither man had great political skill. Gómez, like Che Guevara, was a foreigner, a Dominican. The theme of the war was announced by Céspedes himself: "Better . . . that Cuba should be free even if we have to burn every vestige of civilization." Quoted in Thomas, *Cuba*, p. 255.
11 Ibid., p. 254.
12 The constitutional convention which was convened in April 1869 drew up a model representative democracy for Cuba, but it also espoused annexation to the United States—an inauspicious beginning for the incipient republic. Ibid., p. 250.

guerrilla armies—a pattern that a century later Régis Debray would recommend (and later repudiate) for all revolutionary movements in Latin America, though he believed it had first emerged in the Cuban insurgency against Batista.[13] But the domination of any political movement by the military is hardly conducive to the development of liberal democracy, much less the civilian's authority over the soldier.

Finally, the war ended as it began, on an ambiguous note. With order at home and fresh troops in the field, Spain forced the rebels into their last strongholds in Oriente province. At the same time it offered generous peace terms which amounted to amnesty for the rebel army and exile for its leaders. Many of them accepted what came to be known as the Pact of Zanjón, and even Antonio Maceo, an old revolutionary who still insisted on independence and abolition, was forced to accept exile after a few months more of struggle.

It has been argued that, whatever the cost of the Ten Years' War, it did arouse a sense of nationhood and from it there emerged a Cuban people who were ready and able to take on the responsibility of self-government.[14] This is true, though often overstated in a way that minimizes the influence of the Cubans who continued to look to Spain or the United States as the island's protector. Those well-established elements would flourish long after the end of the war, unlike the Loyalists in this country after 1783. Nevertheless, the quality of Cuban nationalism deserves another look.

The Rise of Cuban Nationalism. Island peoples tend to achieve a sense of nationhood early: the English, the Japanese, the Icelanders, and the Irish did.[15] But for Cuba this was not the case. Though settled a century before North America, it did not gain independence for more than a century after the American revolution. Furthermore, Cuba legally remained a protectorate until 1934, and some contend that the full flowering of Cuban nationalism did not occur until Fidel Castro's assumption of power. It might be added that long-

---

[13] See his *Revolution in the Revolution?*, trans. Bobbye Ortiz (New York: MR Press, 1967). Debray has now in large part repudiated his old views. See his *La Critique des Armes* (Paris: Seuil, 1974), vol. 1. For a brilliant critique of the *Critique*, see Walter Laqueur, "In Dubious Battle," *Times Literary Supplement*, 1 August 1975.

[14] See Thomas, *Cuba*, p. 270, for example.

[15] Those who see few barriers separating the U.S. from Cuba might consider the current status of Anglo-Irish relations. After five centuries there is less than profound friendship between these two peoples. It is true that Britain's record exceeds anything the United States ever did on Cuba, either in terms of duration or severity. Moreover, America does not face the problem of a loyalist enclave on the island. Guantánamo is no Belfast. Nevertheless, the analogy is suggestive: rapprochement will not be easy.

delayed nationhood after a prolonged period of frustrated nationalism often has unpleasant results: one might cite Germany and Italy in the last century, China and innumerable other instances in the present one.

Besides being late in development and limited in appeal, Cuban nationalism had little to build on. Was there a Cuban people after all? There had been no significant pre-Columbian past, nor was there a surviving indigenous culture around which intellectuals could construct a plausible national myth.[16] Instead, during the colonial period the island had been firmly attached to the metropole and its middle and upper classes disagreed as to whether it aspired to being, in the future, a province of Spain, a state in the North American union, or an independent nation. Moreover, most of Cuba's inhabitants, thanks in large part to slavery, were very much removed from any participation in national life whatsoever.[17]

The people who did become the spokesmen for the new Cuban nationalism that emerged during the Ten Years' War were the eastern planters, soon joined by the Havana intellectuals, their students, and the liberal element of the clergy. This relative isolation of the country's nationalists gave Cuban nationalism a quality it still possesses: unyielding, romantic, xenophobic. This xenophobia was directed mainly at Spain, but even before independence hatred of the foreigner also embraced the American.

Cuban nationalism, especially in its anti-American aspect, is inextricably linked with José Martí, the prolific writer and revolutionary-in-exile who became the cult figure of Cuban history. Only Fidel Castro, a far better student of Martí than of Lenin, has anything like Martí's importance as a nationalist symbol. Since much can be learned about a society from what it chooses to celebrate,[18] a glance at his life and work are worth our while.

José Martí. Martí (1853–1895) reflects that odd mixture of elements that makes Cuban nationalism so distinctive. His parents were not Cuban. His father was a Spaniard (like Castro's) and his mother a Canary Islander.[19] Martí became involved in radical politics at the age of sixteen, setting the mold for future generations of young

---

[16] In Latin America both Mexico and Paraguay's Indian cultures have contributed to making each a distinct people. In Peru and Bolivia the Indian peoples have remained outside national life.

[17] C. A. M. Hennessy, "The Roots of Cuban Nationalism," *International Affairs,* July 1963, p. 346.

[18] Martí's centenary was marked by the publication of 500 articles. Ibid., p. 354.

[19] The biographical facts were culled from Thomas, *Cuba,* pp. 293-317. No critical biography of Martí exists, though of course several detailed eulogies are available.

Cubans, and was soon arrested and sentenced to six years of hard labor. Like Castro, too, he served only part of his sentence. He then went into exile, first to Spain where he earned a law degree and then to the United States where he remained for fourteen years. During his adult life, he returned to his homeland only on three brief occasions. On the first two visits he found life in Havana intolerable and left. His final visit was a secret landing to resume the war of independence, a brave, perhaps foolhardy, act that ended in his death at the hands of the Spanish army. His Cuban patriotism, though genuine and deeply felt, was a product of his great imagination, seldom touching ground with the Cuban reality. This interpretation of Martí, naturally, is controversial and no doubt unacceptable to most Cubans. But it does help explain the kind of nationalism that actually developed and culminated in the work of Fidel Castro.

Martí may have been a romantic in thought and deed, but he was also a capable organizer, managing to bring together the disparate groups of Cuban nationalists in exile in New York and Florida—a feat never accomplished before and not duplicated until Fidel Castro brought together all revolutionary groups at the end of the *batistiato*.

Martí's importance to Americans, of course, was his opinion of this country. He lived in the United States for fourteen years, but his feelings toward it were ambivalent at best.[20] On the one hand, Martí did admire our working democracy (although he felt, probably correctly, that it could not be transplanted to Latin America). On the other hand, he became critical of American "materialism" and grew fearful of the United States's expanding economic power—two themes that quickly became the staples of the Spanish American intelligentsia.

One other theme, however, did tie Cuba directly to the future of Latin America. Martí felt his native land should act as a barrier to North American expansionism. If Cuba could maintain its independence, despite its diminutive size and proximity to the goliath Anglo-Saxon republic, then all Latin Americans, like so many Israelites, would rally around their David and fend off the philistines of the North. In short, Cuba by its example would inspire the quarreling Spanish-speaking republics to unite and fulfill Bolívar's grand vision of a powerful Spanish American nation. Martí's hope for Cuba as model and perhaps leader became a principal ingredient of Cuban nationalism and would emerge again in its most virulent form under the aegis of Fidel Castro.

---

[20] It should be pointed out that Martí was never content with any country he lived in, including Cuba. His restless, romantic temperament made that impossible.

The United States and Cuba

American concern for Cuba goes back to the early years of the republic. President Jefferson, for example, offered to buy the island from Spain in 1807 rather than let it fall into the hands of the British or French.[21] Jefferson's proposal was not some historical quirk, best forgotten. It was, in fact, his considered answer to a question he thought vital to the United States—namely, who would control Cuba?

Why should he and so many of his generation think Cuba so important? The best reply to that question came from John Quincy Adams. Writing in 1823 as secretary of state, Adams called Cuba "an object of transcendent importance to the political and commercial interests of our Union." He continued:

> Its commanding position with reference to the Gulf of Mexico and the West India seas; the character of its population; its situation midway between our southern coast and the island of San Domingo; its safe and capacious harbor of the Havana, fronting a long line of our shores destitute of the same advantage; the nature of its productions and of its wants, furnishing the supplies and needing the returns of a commerce immensely profitable and mutually beneficial; give it an importance in the sum of our national interests, with which that of no other foreign territory can be compared, and little inferior to that which binds the different members of this Union together.[22]

---

[21] Isaac Cox, "The Pan-American Policy of Jefferson and Wilkinson," *Mississippi Valley Historical Review*, September 1914, pp. 212-39, and Thomas, *Cuba*, p. 88. Jefferson, sixteen years later in a reply to President Monroe's request for advice on South America, briefly alluded to the region and then pressed on to an obviously favorite topic: Cuba. He wrote: "I candidly confess, that I have ever looked on Cuba as the most interesting addition which could ever be made to our system of States. The control which, with Florida Point, this island would give us over the Gulf of Mexico, and the countries and isthmus bordering on it, as well as all those whose waters flow into it, would fill up the measure of our political well-being." But Jefferson adds a cautionary note: "Yet, as I am sensible that this can never be obtained, even with her own consent, but by war; and its independence, which is our second interest (and especially its independence of England), can be secured without it, I have no hesitation in abandoning my first wish to future chances, and accepting its independence with peace and friendship of England, rather than its association, at the expense of war and her enmity." Letter to James Monroe, 24 October 1823, in Adrienne Koch and William Peden, eds., *The Life and Selected Writings of Thomas Jefferson* (New York: Modern Library, 1944), pp. 709-10.

[22] Quoted from Secretary of State John Quincy Adams's written instructions to Hugh Nelson, 28 April 1823, in Worthington Chauncey Ford, ed., *The Writings of John Quincy Adams* (New York: Macmillan Co., 1917), vol. 7, p. 372.

12

Cuba was important for national security and commerce.[23] It was no wonder that the United States would have welcomed the peaceful acquisition of the island. But under no circumstances could the United States allow, without war, a transfer of Cuba to England or France. If American acquisition proved impossible, then continued Spanish control would be acceptable (although hardly desirable) until the Cubans could win their own independence. That this future independence would mean close ties with this country was accepted here as inevitable and hardly shameful. Nevertheless, Jefferson was also committed to independence for all people capable of self-government. In a letter written ten days before his death, he wrote: "May [our Declaration of Independence] be to the world what I believe it will be (to some parts sooner, to others later, but finally to all) the signal of arousing men to burst the chains under which monkish ignorance and superstition had persuaded them to bind themselves, and to assume the blessings and security of self government." [24]

But despite this consensus about Cuba's importance to the United States and despite its proximity, wealth, and weakness—despite even the wishes of Cuba's leading men—the island did not, in Adams's famous metaphor, fall like an apple "severed by the tempest from its native tree" to its natural resting place: the North American union.[25]

What did emerge after 1825 was an increasingly tangled relationship, with neither Cuba nor the United States achieving what it wanted. And the problem was compounded by the fact that neither had a clear idea of what it expected from the other. The result, of course, was that Cuba never peacefully integrated itself into the American union, nor did it ever achieve self-sustaining independence.[26] For the United States, Cuba became a classic worst case:

---

[23] Early American preoccupation with Cuba as a security problem was not idle. During the War of 1812, England through its alliance with Spain used Cuban ports to attack the U.S. mainland. Thomas, *Cuba*, p. 87.

[24] Letter to Roger C. Weightman, 24 June 1826, in Koch and Peden, eds., *Selected Writings of Thomas Jefferson*, p. 729. I cannot resist quoting the rest of the passage: "That form which we have substituted, restores the free right to the unbounded exercise of reason and freedom of opinion. All eyes are opened, or opening, to the rights of man. The general spread of the light of science has already laid open to every view the palpable truth, that the mass of mankind has not been born with saddles on their backs, nor a favored few booted and spurred, ready to ride them legitimately, by the grace of God. These are grounds of hope for others."

[25] Adams to Nelson, in Ford, ed., *Writings of John Quincy Adams*, p. 373.

[26] Legally Cuba was not fully sovereign until the repeal of the Platt Amendment in 1934.

it fell under the control of a major foreign power—a development which our first generation of leaders had been prepared to go to war to prevent—and at the same time (especially after 1898) we could not decide between making Cuba a protectorate and letting it go its own way.

In Search of a Policy, 1825–1898. Both Jefferson and Adams counselled patience regarding Cuba. Either it would become part of the Union of its own accord or it would achieve independence. But despite Adams's confidence in the laws of political gravity, Cuba continued its "unnatural connection" for another seventy-five years, breaking it only with the help of United States military intervention. The course of Cuban history was not, in short, what Jefferson or Adams had expected. What went wrong?

To be sure, Americans did not lose interest in Cuba. In the two decades before the American Civil War no less than three U.S. presidents made offers to Spain for the purchase of the island.[27] The push for annexation came from two directions. In Cuba, wealthy slaveholders feared a revolt or sudden emancipation ordered by the Spaniards—who found it useful to divide the creole camp by threatening just that. At the same time, Spain was under pressure from Britain and France to end the slave trade and even slavery itself.[28] Fear of "another Haiti," meanwhile, made the Cuban elite docile or desperate to join the United States.

In this country, the pressure for annexation came from the South and was based on two main arguments. First, the island would add one or more slave states to the Union. Second, annexation would prevent the end of slavery in Cuba which, it was felt, would threaten slavery in this country. Fear of the so-called "Africanization of

---

[27] Hard pressed for funds, Queen Isabella II was tempted to accept the offer from the Pierce administration, but an untimely revolution interrupted the negotiations. The other presidential offers came from James Polk and James Buchanan. Lincoln, it should be noted, refused to make any such offer as long as slavery continued in Cuba, despite Secretary of State William Seward's Machiavellian suggestion that purchase of Cuba would keep the South in the Union. See Thomas, *Cuba*, pp. 207-32, and Lester D. Langley, *The Cuban Policy of the United States* (New York: John Wiley, 1968).

[28] The motives of Europe's grand powers were, at best, mixed. On the one hand, especially in England, there was a moral revolt against slavery. On the other, each country had ended slavery in its Caribbean possessions and was anxious to avoid competition with a slave economy. But pressure from England and France was intermittent and not nearly as persistent as Britain's efforts to stop the trade between Africa and Brazil. The reason was simple: neither England nor France was willing to go to war with Spain over the matter. See Urban, "Africanization of Cuba," pp. 29-45, and Thomas, *Cuba*, p. 231.

Cuba" produced some of the most virulent political bombast in our history.[29] One of the best examples came from the infamous Ostend manifesto written by three impatient American diplomats who felt that Spain was stalling in its negotiations with the United States on Cuba. The preamble read in part:

> We should be unworthy of our gallant forefathers and commit base treason against our posterity if Cuba were to be Africanized and become another Santo Domingo [that is, Haiti] with all its attendant horrors to the white race, and suffer the flames to extend to our neighboring shores, seriously to endanger or actually destroy the fabric of our Union.[30]

Cuban annexation was not, however, a narrow sectional interest. Non-Southerners like Buchanan, Pierce, and Stephen Douglas also favored it since acquiring Cuba fitted into their own nationalist-expansionist philosophy which found expression in the Young America movement of the 1850s.

The move to annex Cuba resulted not only in more or less peaceful purchase bids.[31] Armed expeditions involving both Cubans and Americans were also prepared, but enjoyed no more success than the purchase attempts.[32] The most disastrous of these forays involved 400 Cubans, Americans, and Hungarians led by General Narciso López in August 1850. The landing at Bahía Honda was botched, the expedition divided, the participants subsequently captured and executed or sentenced to hard labor. What's more, the Cuban under-

---

[29] Urban, "Africanization of Cuba," pp. 29-30.

[30] Other voices were even more strident. The *New Orleans Creole Courier* trumpeted on 27 January 1855: "This full-blooded Anglo-American race is destined to sweep over the world with the might of a tornado. The Hispano-Morescan (sic) race will quail." And the *New Orleans Delta*, 3 January 1853, was no less fulsome: "For the bastard Latin of their nation cannot stand for any time against the conquering power of the robust and hearty English. . . . Their political sentimentalism and anarchical tendencies follow rapidly after the language and by degrees the absorption of the people becomes complete—all due to inevitable dominance of the American mind over an inferior race." Quoted in Thomas, *Cuba*, p. 210.

[31] Pierce's appointment of Pierre Soulé, a French lawyer transplanted to New Orleans who had adopted the Southern cause, as ambassador to Spain was one of Pierce's more imprudent decisions. Soulé was already a notorious annexationist and his nomination was roughly equivalent in sensitivity to a hypothetical Eisenhower selection of Senator Joseph McCarthy for the ambassadorship in Moscow.

[32] Robert E. Lee was offered command of one such expedition and wisely refused it. Thomas, *Cuba*, p. 214.

ground was smashed just before the landing—another parallel with the no less disastrous Bay of Pigs expedition.[33]

Thus, before the Civil War the clear lines of American policy fashioned in the early days of the republic had become badly blurred by irreconcilable sectional interests and a careless enthusiasm for expansion. Nor did emancipation in this country restore sound policy, although two American statesmen, Hamilton Fish, secretary of state under President Grant, and Grover Cleveland, did their best to keep America out of war over Cuba. Secretary Fish stoutly opposed all schemes of annexation by force. Moreover, he was reluctant to grant belligerency status to the Cuban rebels—a move he correctly believed would have greatly strained relations with Spain. Fish did hope that in time Cuba would gravitate to the United States after resolving its slavery question.[34] Not surprisingly, Fish's quiet diplomacy was vigorously opposed in this country. Although no major power threatened a takeover, Cuba did become an important security question for the expansionists. President Grant apparently hoped for naval bases in either Cuba or Santo Domingo, but was unwilling to take any great risks to obtain them despite the urgings of Secretary of War John Rawlins.[35] Compounding Fish's problem was the familiar pattern of exile politics.[36] On the one hand the exiles lobbied for American intervention during the Ten Years' War, and on the other they prepared armed expeditions on American soil. In most cases the latter were thwarted by official action, and luckily for Fish and his successors the Pact of Zanjón helped end the issue for a decade.

But the Cuba question was not answered. By the 1890s Cleveland and then McKinley came under even greater pressure as a result of a number of new developments. First, the slavery question was resolved when Spain abolished slavery in 1888.[37] Second, a new

---

[33] Besides enlisting the efforts of American adventurers, the Cuban exile groups were not above attempting to solicit direct U.S. intervention by spreading alarming stories that the British (or French) were seeking some form of control over the island. See ibid., p. 207, for just one example.

[34] Fish was persuaded to attempt another round of negotiations with Spain perhaps in an attempt to forestall American recognition of Cuban belligerency. The negotiations revolved around Cuba's paying Spain for its independence through a guaranteed U.S. loan. But in familiar fashion, the Spanish colonial minister leaked word of the talks and the subsequent uproar ended the matter. Ibid., pp. 252-53.

[35] Rawlins's interest in the island was stimulated by his holding of Cuban bonds issued by the New York exiles. Ibid., p. 251.

[36] The exiles already had their allies in the press, especially Horace Greeley of the *New York Tribune*, and the American Congress. But these would not multiply until another decade had passed. Ibid., pp. 256-57.

[37] Ibid., p. 279.

spirit of expansionism swept the country in the last quarter of the nineteenth century. Its spokesmen, such as Senator Albert Beveridge, foresaw a vastly enlarged role for the United States in world affairs. And along with effusions on Anglo-Saxon achievements came a more sober assessment of America's new security needs, which were outlined with great vigor by Captain Alfred Mahan. Moreover, the new mood was not tied to sectional interests this time. A third factor was the fading memory of the Civil War. The new political generation, perhaps typified by Theodore Roosevelt, was eager for a "scrap"— with almost anyone, it seemed—and Spain became the most accessible candidate. Fourth, the Cubans themselves provided a fresh opportunity for American concern by rebelling again in 1895, with the same leaders using the same tactics they had employed in the Ten Years' War.[38] Finally, a new and perhaps decisive factor which pushed American policy off its old track emerged in the 1890s: a shift in popular opinion. The instinctive humanitarianism of literate Americans was aroused by a steady flow of stories depicting Spanish outrages against the Cuban people. That most of these stories were fabricated by Hearst and Pulitzer reporters idling in Havana's hotel bars, of course, does not depreciate the sincerity of the public's reaction, although it did begin a long tradition of bad American coverage of Cuban affairs which has continued to this day.[39]

Despite the pressures, both old and new, for intervention,[40] Cleveland kept the United States from meddling in the Caribbean. He did not grant belligerent status to the rebels, and he did prosecute those who broke the nation's neutrality laws by supplying arms to the insurgents. At the same time his secretary of state, Richard Olney, once again attempted negotiations with Spain. This time, however, the object was not purchase of the island. Instead, Olney argued that the United States wished an end to the Cuban insurrection since its prolongation might draw this country into war with Spain. Olney proposed a compromise: acceptance by all parties of Spain's sovereignty over the island in exchange for Cuban autonomy in local affairs. The Spaniards, already stung by the American press, rejected Olney's note.[41]

---

[38] See above, pp. 7-9.

[39] For another account, which questions the conventional belief that the Spanish-American War belonged to William R. Hearst, see George W. Auxier, "Middle Western Newspapers and the Spanish-American War, 1895-1898," *Mississippi Valley Historical Review*, vol. 26 (1940), pp. 523-34.

[40] After 1895 the Cuban exiles were able to raise more money than ever from rallies held in Madison Square Garden among other places. Thomas, *Cuba*, pp. 331-32.

[41] Ibid., p. 338.

Cautious Cleveland, of course, took a drubbing for not taking vigorous action on Cuba, and one of his congressional critics, William McKinley, became the Republican candidate for the presidency in 1896. But in office McKinley, like John Kennedy sixty years later, turned cautious and managed to avoid any direct reference to Cuba in his inaugural address.[42] Privately, McKinley now indicated his approval of Spanish constitutional reforms on the grounds that this was the most that could be obtained short of war—which he wished increasingly to avoid. This was, of course, precisely the policy that had been fostered by the previous administration.[43] The president, however, could not remain inert, especially since the insurrection seemed without a quick solution. McKinley therefore began pushing two lines of policy. First, he quietly revived the old purchase scheme. The second idea, enunciated in his first State of the Union message (6 December 1897), spelled out the grounds for American concern. Humanitarianism, he argued, impelled the United States to help bring about a "righteous peace" and to do so by force if the Spanish made no progress toward that end.[44]

Neither policy came to anything, and McKinley found himself being pushed into war by events. The first was the so-called de Lôme letter written by the Spanish ambassador in Washington to a friend in New York. The letter pungently described the American president. Unfortunately for de Lôme, it fell into the hands of Cuban exiles who forwarded it to the New York press.[45] Far worse for McKinley's peace policy was the sinking of the *Maine*. Ironically, the president had sent the battleship to Havana in order to protect American life and property, the destruction of which he had feared would draw us into war.[46] To make matters worse, an official U.S. inquiry blamed the Spanish government for the disaster. By the spring of 1898 the

---

[42] McKinley, however, did assure his listeners that this country would "never undertake a war without exhausting all ways of avoiding it." Ibid., p. 342. Meanwhile his secretary of state, former Senator Sherman, long a passionate foe of Spain and friend of Cuba (he had already argued for recognizing the rebels in 1870), likewise turned moderate once he became responsible for his rhetoric.

[43] Ibid., p. 348.

[44] James D. Richardson, *Messages and Papers of the Presidents* (Washington, D.C.: Bureau of National Literature and Art, 1904), p. 36.

[45] The president was described as a weak, popularity-seeking man and a hack politician. See Thomas, *Cuba*, pp. 360-61. Members of the same outraged press, of course, had in their own time called McKinley much worse things.

[46] The president had received highly exaggerated accounts of local unrest from the American consul in Havana, General Fitzhugh Lee, a long-time advocate of vigorous intervention in Cuba. Ibid., pp. 356-58.

sentiment for war in this country was very strong, and McKinley proved unable to resist it.[47]

The New Relationship, 1898–1959. The war itself was short and bitter, not at all the "splendid little war" that John Hay (not Theodore Roosevelt) had anticipated.[48] Casualties were high and the war seemed to lose its purpose as the American army learned to despise its Cuban allies and admire the Spanish enemy. Friction between allies, of course, is nothing new in war, but that brief encounter was the basis for the resentment and anti-Americanism that Fidel Castro could express sixty years later with obvious audience approval. The war also brought another change in our relationship with Cuba. Once Spain was no longer responsible for the ravaged island, the United States had to assume the burden.

The United States, the expansionists hoped, had embarked on a new "large policy," but that policy's relevance to Cuba, aside from a vague desire to prepare the island for independence, was never made clear.[49] In three and a half years of direct military occupation, the American proconsuls, Generals John Brooke and Leonard Wood, began cleaning up the island, reforming laws and the courts, reorganizing the schools, and almost totally ignoring the Cubans.[50] It was,

---

[47] Ironically, those who did oppose war were American property holders in Cuba. Ibid., p. 365. McKinley, it must be said, made one last secret offer to the Spanish government to purchase Cuba. This time, however, a specific sum was mentioned: $300 million. Although the offer was refused, by 9 April 1898 the Spanish government had agreed to most of the American demands including an unconditional armistice, arbitration on the *Maine*, and some form of autonomy for the Cubans. These concessions were virtually ignored by the administration, and on 25 April 1898 Congress declared war. Ibid., pp. 367, 373–77.

[48] Roosevelt knew better: he was there. At one point he wrote Senator Lodge about his fear that the U.S. Army was headed for a "terrible military disaster." Quoted in ibid., p. 395. Even a large part of the jingoist press had turned against the war before it ended.

[49] Most Cubans have long held that they were already able to govern themselves. Indeed, it is an article of faith that U.S. intervention in 1898 was unnecessary—the Cubans were winning *their* war of independence. This thesis, which, of course, is maintained by the present regime, is suspect. By early 1898 the Spanish army had again turned the tide. Furthermore, the Cuban leader, General Maximo Gómez, welcomed American aid, knowing well his own military situation. But in the actual fighting there was little if any effective collaboration—the Cubans remained on the sideline, as they would during the 1962 missile crisis. (See ibid., p. 381 for this insight.) In the meantime, small incidents completely forgotten by Americans, like General Calixto García's nonparticipation in the surrender of Santiago, later became major points of anti-Americanism in Cuban historiography.

[50] General Wood reopened the schools, modeling them after their American counterparts and using U.S. textbooks translated directly into Spanish. More than sixty years later the Cuban educational system was again reorganized along Soviet lines with Russian textbooks directly translated into Spanish.

of course, an odd sort of arrangement. The United States was not occupying a defeated enemy, and therefore did not have the moral certitude in refounding the nation that it was to have in Germany and Japan after World War II. On the other hand, the Cubans desperately needed help. The four-year war had brought great destruction through the tactics of the guerrillas and the reconcentration policy of the Spanish. As many as 300,000 Cubans had died—over 10 percent of the population—and the economy, especially sugar farming, was in ruins. Moreover, the country was in debt by over $200 million. The best that can be said for the American occupation was that the material aid given was generous. The United States, moreover, did withdraw after a few years with no serious intention of annexation. Indeed, through the Foraker Amendment the military government was forbidden from granting concessions to American business. Finally, the occupation authorities did manage to avoid fresh insurgency against their government of the sort that occurred in the Philippines. The American withdrawal, however, was conditional, guided by the provisions of the Platt Amendment. That famous amendment, so deeply resented by all Cubans since the beginning of their republic, established a rough sort of American protectorate over the island. Cuba was to be unoccupied, but not entirely sovereign. The amendment (which, in fact, was a treaty between the United States and Cuba) stipulated four major terms. First, Cuba could not place itself under the control of any foreign power or provide it with military bases. Second, foreign loans could not be contracted without visible means to repay them. Violation of this provision was a certain formula for outside intervention, as the author of the Roosevelt Corollary well knew. Third, Platt gave the United States the right to intervene if Cuban independence or internal order were threatened. Finally, it provided for the leasing of future naval stations to the United States.[51]

This protectorate, though well intended, did not help the Cubans learn how to govern themselves, nor did it improve their sense of self-esteem. The United States, in fact, soon became a kind of final arbiter, the effective supreme court of the island. When factions struggled for power through a corrupt electoral system, the losers immediately cried fraud and demanded some sort of American intervention, and the Americans often complied. When civil war threatened, as it did in 1906, the United States did physically intervene in an attempt to build a lasting constitutional order.

---

[51] Charles E. Chapman, *A History of the Cuban Republic* (New York: Macmillan Co., 1927), pp. 136-37.

But neither intervention nor diplomacy brought orderly, much less democratic, government to Cuba. And the repeal of Platt in 1934 established in law what had been true in fact since the middle 1920s when General Machado had established his iron-fisted dictatorship—the first in independent Cuba's history.[52] The Americans would no longer attempt to guide the Cubans toward democracy or even political decency. The exasperation of American policy makers was perhaps best expressed by Harry F. Guggenheim after years of service as ambassador in Havana: "There has been a laissez-faire policy and there has been a tutorial policy; there have been lectures, admonitions and threats; there has been a policy based on a strict construction of the Platt Amendment; and there has been a policy based on broad construction."[53] And as Guggenheim well knew, nothing worked. It was a classic case of cross-cultural confusion and frustration. Cubans were mystified by American values and Americans were equally baffled by Cuban mores. No wonder that the United States engaged in little outright intervention from 1933 until 1959—the quarter-century which coincided with the Batista era. Cuba, of course, was finally free of the Spanish connection, and no other foreign power threatened it. But our attempt to make them like us was an ignominious failure.

In sum, the United States did not occupy Cuba long enough to carry out the fundamental reorganization needed to prepare a war-torn and corrupt society for orderly, perhaps even democratic, self-rule. Nor did this country adopt the opposite policy of scrupulous nonintervention, until bitter experience had taught its leaders better—and firm habits of Yankee baiting had already been acquired by the Cubans. Rather, the United States chose a middle course through the Platt Amendment of limited intervention for the Cubans' own good. Aspiring to be a favorite aunt, we earned the reputation (in Cuba at least) of a wicked stepmother.

Yet while our political manipulation seemed to do little good, our economic ties were changing the island for the better. Or were they?

The Ties that Bound. Nothing has provoked more outrage in Cuba over the years, or more self-flagellation in the United States, than the business of the business that developed between the two countries.

---

[52] Henry Wriston, "A Historical Perspective," in John Plank, ed., *Cuba and the United States: Long Range Perspectives* (Washington, D.C.: The Brookings Institution, 1967), p. 17.

[53] Quoted in Wriston, from Harry F. Guggenheim, *The United States and Cuba* (New York: Macmillan Co., 1934), p. 160.

21

It could hardly have been otherwise. In no other country was the American presence so obvious. By 1960 the U.S. investment was concentrated in the key Cuban industries: sugar, tobacco, cattle ranching, and mining, but it also involved manufacturing, public utilities, insurance, and banking. Moreover, 80 percent of Cuba's imports in 1957 came from the United States—everything from toothpaste to tractors. Quite understandably, dependency and exploitation soon became common themes in Cuban economic literature.

That such an intimate connection should have developed is cause for neither surprise nor regret. The two countries, as Jefferson well appreciated, were complementary: the United States with its temperate agriculture and burgeoning industry, and Cuba, tropical and, unlike Haiti, extremely fertile. These two economies were better examples of comparative advantage than Ricardo's England and Portugal. And despite Spanish mercantilism, commerce between the neighbors was already flourishing by the early nineteenth century. In 1826, for example, 783 of the 964 ships visiting Havana were American.[54] The two most typical products of exchange were American flour and Cuban sugar. Nevertheless, sugar did not dominate Cuban-American trade until half a century later when Cuba, still under Spanish control, became dependent on the American market. That dependency was a result of the rapidly growing European sugar beet industry which satisfied continental demand by the mid-1880s. Even Spain by 1898 produced more sugar than it could consume.[55] Not surprisingly, four years before Cuba's break from Spain, the United States was already absorbing 87 percent of its exports and supplying the island with 38 percent of its imports.[56] That pattern continued unchanged, except for a steady rise in the U.S. percentage of Cuban imports, until 1960.[57]

Trade was only half of the dependency equation—and the lesser half in the eyes of Cuban nationalists. The other, American invest-

---

[54] Thomas, *Cuba*, p. 194.

[55] Ibid., p. 272.

[56] Ibid., p. 289.

[57] From 38 percent the U.S. percentage of Cuban imports rose to 80 percent. The percentage of exports dipped a bit, from 87 percent down to 69 percent in 1957, making the island gradually less dependent on the United States. J. Wilner Sundelson, "A Business Perspective," in Plank, ed., *Cuba and the United States*, p. 100. Percentages, however, conceal one obvious but often overlooked fact: the enormous increase in trade volume. In 1894 Cuba's exports to the United States totalled $98,000 while American exports were worth $38,508. Thomas, *Cuba*, p. 289. In 1957, U.S. exports were valued at $581 million and Cuban exports were $498 million. Central Intelligence Agency, "Cuba: Foreign Trade," *Intelligence Handbook*, July 1957, Table 3, p. 7, and Table 8, p. 12.

ment, was an enormous presence in Cuban life, and consequently became the target of every demagogue and careless economist the island produced—and it produced these in great profusion. U.S. direct investment totalled only $30 million in 1895, but had grown to $956 million by 1960—the second largest total direct U.S. investment in Latin America after Venezuela's.[58] The extent of this investment presence was possibly unique in international relations. But before examining the issue of exploitation, we must explore one nexus between trade and investment in the Cuban economy: the Cuban sugar industry.

That most distinctly Cuban of products was dominated not by American capitalists but by Cuban planters until the twentieth century. In 1902, for example, of a total of $100 million in American capital on the island only a quarter was invested in sugar, while the tobacco industry received $45 million.[59] But the reciprocity treaty of 1903 changed the investment profile. The treaty gave Cuba a preference on exports to the United States by setting the tariff 20 percent below that which applied for other countries. That comparative edge stimulated American investment in the industry especially suited to Cuba—sugar.[60] Thus, by the end of World War I (which, in turn, had stimulated a sugar boom) U.S. companies were responsible for 50 percent of the crop. After the boom collapsed in the summer of 1920, an even larger share of the industry was purchased by American banks foreclosing on bankrupt mills.[61] By 1928, American-owned canefields produced 70 percent of the zafra. A decade later that percentage had dropped to 56 percent and by 1958, the year before Fidel Castro's arrival in Havana, it had dropped again to perhaps 35 percent.[62]

---

[58] Thomas, *Cuba*, pp. 290, 1057. Comparative figures on U.S. investment on a per capita basis in 1960 are the following: Venezuela—$342.5; Cuba—$138.6; Mexico—$22.8; Brazil—$13.5. Investment figures are calculated from the *Statistical Abstract of the United States, 1968* and *World Almanac, 1963*, pp. 332, 339, 386.

[59] Thomas, *Cuba*, p. 466. U.S. investors purchased at least half a dozen sugar estates between 1892 and 1898, and although these tended to be large, they still represented only a fraction of what Spaniards and Cubans owned. Thomas, *Cuba*, p. 290.

[60] Ibid., pp. 469-70.

[61] In 1921 alone National City Bank took over sixty sugar mills after their owners declared bankruptcy. Ibid., p. 551.

[62] Ibid., p. 541, and Theodore Draper, *Castroism, Theory and Practice* (New York: Praeger, 1965), p. 109. In 1937, ownership of the Cuban sugar industry was as follows: United States, sixty-nine mills, 56 percent of production; Cuba, fifty mills, 20 percent of production; Spain, thirty-six mills, 17 percent of production; Canada, eleven mills; Britain, four mills; France, two mills; and the Netherlands,

Direct American ownership of the sugar mills aside, Cuban exports continued to depend on the U.S. market. In fact, sugar sales became institutionalized between 1934 and 1960 through the American sugar quota system under which foreign and domestic suppliers were given fixed shares in the U.S. market. The quota was based on producers' shares of the market between 1931 and 1933—base years which happened to favor the American sugar beet industry. The actual size of exports to the United States was determined by the secretary of agriculture's annual estimate of the market for sugar and the limits on imported sugar needed to keep the high-cost domestic beet producers in business, and the American price for sugar was above the world price. These two factors—a guaranteed market and a high price—meant for Cuba more foreign exchange and continued dependence on the American market.

This very high American profile in Cuba's principal industry had both great advantages and drawbacks. In the first place, American investment was substantially responsible for the modernization of the industry in the 1920s. Moreover, the new American-owned *centrales* were located in previously undeveloped rural areas, which helped reduce the growing gap between Havana and the countryside.[63] The American market also guaranteed a secure outlet for Cuban sugar and, while nationalist critics have always called this "servitude," even in retrospect there seem to have been few, if any, substantial markets available outside the United States. As far as the Soviet Union is concerned, that country was in no position to buy large quantities of sugar in the 1920s and 1930s, even if it had found such purchases politically advantageous. The other nationalist charge—that U.S. domination of sugar prevented needed diversification—is questionable. First, diversification had been taking place (though not in exports), and when a radical regime intent on industrialization failed in its attempt to diversify the Cuban economy, it discovered the socialist law of comparative advantage which stated that Cuba was most suited to growing sugar cane.[64]

The cruder anti-American economic argument (still heard from the highest possible source in Cuba) that U.S. investment actually

---

two mills with the last four accounting for 7 percent of production. Thomas, *Cuba*, p. 708.

[63] Thomas, *Cuba*, p. 708.

[64] The extreme policy of neglecting the sugar industry (1959-1963) ultimately bred its opposite. By the late 1960s the Cuban economy was sacrificed for no discernible reason to the production of more sugar than ever—10 million tons. "Only" 8.5 million were harvested—this was itself a record—but in the process the rest of the economy received a blow that would have prompted nationalist cries of outrage if it had been the result of American investment.

impoverished Cuba is easily dismissed. The Cubas of 1898 and 1959 hardly resembled one another. From a level of almost unbelievable wretchedness, the standard of living had become fairly comfortable for a majority of Cubans. That it did not do more was due to a large number of factors, mostly unrelated to American investment.

The less crude argument that foreign ownership of such a large part of the Cuban economy left vital economic decisions to outsiders has much greater merit. Cuba did suffer because of it. And Cuba also suffered when U.S. trade legislation became restrictive in the 1930s. But it is debatable whether an economy entirely controlled by Cubans would have been substantially better off. Geography dictated a close tie with the American market in those years. Cuba would have followed the same ups and downs it experienced, even without heavy American investment.[65]

Another charge, less frequently heard, contains more truth. That is that the very nature of the American enterprise prevented Cubans from achieving an identity which would have fostered a sense of nationhood. This cultural (rather than strictly economic) loss is keenly appreciated by the current regime, and it can be dated to the nineteenth century when the old Cuban oligarchy lost its grip on society after the trauma of war, occupation, and independence. The absence of indigenous leadership left Cuba unprepared to face the onslaught of the Yankee entrepreneur, who promoted and profited from Cuban progress but who could not make it seem really Cuban.

---

[65] Even Fidel Castro has recently hinted that this is the case. In his 26 July 1975 speech in Santa Clara, Cuba, he acknowledged that militantly socialist Cuba is still not free of outside, non-Communist influence: "Our future will not be free of difficulties and obstacles. We live in a world with many problems. There is a crisis in the capitalist world economy. One way or another, it also affects us. We depend a great deal on the price of sugar. A large portion of our sugar is to be sold to the U.S.S.R. in the next five-year period, with high and stable prices. But another portion—also important—has to be marketed in the capitalist and nonsocialist world. And prices, as you know, go up and go down. The prices that never go down are the prices of imports, the prices of industrialized products. But the prices of the products of underdeveloped nations other than petroleum go up and go down, and most of the time they go down more than they go up.

"Thus today the price of sugar is a mere 25 percent of what it was a few months ago. That is why we will have limitations on our raw materials, imports and financial resources. This means that we may be unable to advance in the next five-year period at the same pace as we have during the past five-year period. But we will continue to advance. Despite all difficulties we will advance." Radio Havana, 26 July 1975, as reported in *Foreign Broadcast Information Service (FBIS) Daily Report, Latin America*, 27 July 1975.

3
FIDEL CASTRO AND THE UNITED STATES: THE SMALL POWER FACES THE SUPERPOWER

Fidel Castro Ruz, commander in chief and prime minister of the Provisional Revolutionary Government of Cuba, occupies a unique position in the history of the Americas. He has remained in power longer than any other self-declared enemy of the United States. At the age of forty-seven he will preside over the negotiations that will establish the new relationship with the United States, and his personal rule could conceivably extend into the twenty-first century.[1]

At those crucial negotiations, then, the United States will be dealing with the same man (surrounded by, to a large extent, the same entourage) whom it proved incapable of handling or even understanding over a dozen years ago. For this reason it would be wise to analyze what went wrong in Cuban-American relations and discover how much was the result of mistakes we could have avoided, how much the inevitable result of lasting differences. This review is not a simple plea for greater understanding of the Castro regime. Too often "understanding" is merely the polite word for indiscriminate acceptance. Instead, the problem of renewing relations must be put into its immediate historical context and our options assessed in the light of the limits already imposed on us.

Small Power versus Superpower

Short of outright war, Cuban-American relations since 1959 could hardly have been more hostile. This fact can be partly understood in terms of the difficulty small nations have always had in getting along

---

[1] Fidel Castro has already outlasted four American presidents.

with large powers—especially when they are near neighbors.[2] Indeed, the basic pattern of big power-little power relationships probably indicates some of the limitations to any easy rapprochement between Cuba and the United States. Let us begin by applying a theoretical model of small-power behavior to the Cuban case.

Small-Power Behavior. Robert Rothstein has argued that the actions of small powers are not those of great powers "writ small," but follow a logic of their own to satisfy the very special needs of small powers.[3] Thus, Cuba's conduct should resemble Belgium's more often than that of the Soviet Union.[4] This useful insight helps to explain aspects of Cuban behavior that are baffling to American observers, including observers sympathetic to the revolution.

According to Rothstein, the role of the small power has changed since the early nineteenth century. By the end of the Napoleonic wars a formal operating principle in international relations had emerged: "the Great Powers, in concert, were to decide; the Small Powers were to obey."[5] In the twentieth century, especially after World War I, the position of the small powers improved despite their continued decline in military strength relative to the great powers.[6] They have, in short, more freedom to maneuver.

Yet the central characteristic of the small power remained its overriding concern with survival. All states, big and little, have security problems, but for the small power security is *the* problem, much more immediate and dangerous. Leaders tend to perceive any threat as a total threat. Furthermore, security for the small power is, as

---

[2] The prophet Isaiah warned Israel (a small power) against any alliance with Egypt (a major power) in Isaiah, Chapters 30 and 31: "Woe to them that go down to Egypt for help [against the Assyrians]; and stay on horses, and trust in chariots, because they are many; and in horsemen, because they are strong; but they look not unto the Holy One of Israel, neither seek the Lord!" Isa. 31: 1 (KJV).

[3] Robert L. Rothstein, *Alliances and Small Powers* (New York: Columbia University Press, 1968), pp. 2-7.

[4] Or if not bourgeois Belgium, most certainly North Korea, North Vietnam, and Albania. Fidel Castro seemed to recognize this in his quest for close relations with North Korea and North Vietnam through the last part of the 1960s.

[5] Rothstein, *Alliances*, p. 13.

[6] Ibid., pp. 20-21. Rothstein's reasons for this improvement are the following: "The continuing growth of an internationalist ethic was of some significance. The exhaustion of the Great Powers after the war was also important. So, too, was the increasing number of Small Powers and the decreasing number of Great Powers. Finally, as the last point suggests, the peculiar nature of the power configuration just before and just after the First World War should not be forgotten: for different reasons each granted many small powers a new status which was difficult to rescind."

Rothstein puts it, "a total requirement only for itself."[7] Therefore, the small power operates within a much narrower margin of safety, and its leaders are constrained to avoid mistakes. They are also compelled to concentrate on "short-run and local matters to the exclusion of, or at least detriment of, any concern for long-run stability."[8] The major powers, of course, tend to concentrate on long-range questions, including the strategic effect of weapon systems that may not even be deployed for another decade.

The small powers' obsession with survival shrinks their range of options. One possibility is to appear detached, disinterested, and insignificant and therefore not worth occupying, annexing, or even plundering.[9] A second ploy is neutrality or nonalignment. A variation on the first attitude, neutrality is invested with far more moral fervor.[10] Its practicality varies, however, in relation to a country's distance from the scene of struggle. Geographically, New Zealand can afford neutrality; Belgium in 1939 clearly could not. A third choice is for the small power to demand—steadily, even shrilly— formal equality, the recognition by others of its right to exist. Israel comes first to mind (along with its mirror image, Palestine). The perfect forum for this demand is any international organization dominated numerically by small powers.[11] Even there, however, this approach is rarely sufficient to protect the small power. The League of Nations did not protect Ethiopia in 1935, nor did the United Nations assist the Czechs in 1968.

The fourth and most viable option open to small powers is alliance. This choice itself may be subdivided: a small power may align itself with a great power in a strictly bilateral arrangement or it may seek a defense arrangement with other small powers. The latter has obvious advantages (including the unlikelihood of being swallowed by one's peers), but it has even more serious drawbacks. The chief one, according to Alfred Cobban, is that "the combination of any number of weak states does not make a strong one."[12] Little

---

[7] Ibid., p. 24.

[8] Ibid., p. 25. Rothstein quotes the Greek dictator of the 1920s, Metaxas, to the effect that muddling through was a luxury allowed only to the great powers.

[9] Ibid., pp. 25-26.

[10] Ibid., pp. 26-27 and pp. 30-34. Insignificance, of course, may only gain for the small power the privilege granted Ulysses by the Cyclops: to be devoured last.

[11] The Latin American states since the First Pan-American Conference (1889-1890) have placed a priority on the recognition by all member states that each state is equal to all the rest and its sovereignty inviolable. They have had remarkable success in having their views accepted on paper at least.

[12] Alfred Cobban, *National Self-Determination* (London: Oxford University Press, 1945), p. 178, and quoted in Rothstein, *Alliances*, p. 117.

ententes, in brief, have rarely terrified the world. Small powers have more often attached themselves to great powers. They have tended to select allies which are "powerful enough to offer substantial material support; and do not possess interests which preclude the use of that power in behalf of the alliance."[13] In addition, an ally should be neither too near a neighbor nor so remote as to be ineffective. Finally, it is important but not vital that an ally share a country's basic ideological outlook.[14] The one great problem with adopting a great power protector is the risk of becoming a mere appendage of it.[15]

Small powers, then, are different from great powers not in degree but in kind. Their problem of survival is far more acute and immediate than that of any great power. Their choices are restricted and never completely satisfying. The temptation in foreign policy is to move from option to option—from alliance to neutrality and back to alliance, perhaps with another ally.[16] At best, solutions are partial, often hastily improvised and nervously executed.

Cuba as a Small Power. This analysis, based largely on the experience of European small powers during the last two centuries, throws new light on Cuban foreign policy since 1959 and helps explain the difficulties U.S. policy makers will have in resuming relations with Cuba. Let us begin with the master premise underlying small-power behavior: the will to survive. That the security of Cuba and its regime has been Castro's paramount concern is obvious enough even to the casual student of Cuban affairs. And this has been the case since the beginning of the Castro era. But it is also clear that this overriding factor was dealt with very differently by earlier Cuban governments. As we have seen, nineteenth-century Cuban revolutionaries believed their object was annexation to the United States. Why the change in perception?

The short answer is that Castro became convinced (or was convinced by others)[17] that the revolution he thought necessary would

---

[13] Rothstein, *Alliances*, pp. 60-61.

[14] Ibid., p. 60.

[15] Ibid., p. 61. Beyond seeking a powerful ally, the small power can develop a strong army, which discourages enemies bent on casual conquest and proves to the ally that it is serious about surviving.

[16] The sudden shifts in Thailand's foreign policy after the collapse of Cambodia and South Vietnam appear to follow the classic small-power pattern of behavior outlined above.

[17] Castro himself alluded to this by stating publicly in a speech on 21 January 1959 that "there are people behind me who are more radical than myself," and then proceeding to mention his brother Raul by name. Quoted in Andrés Suárez, *Cuba, Castroism and Communism, 1959-1966* (Cambridge: MIT Press, 1967), p. 36n.

never be accepted by this country. Meeting the American threat soon became the regime's chief preoccupation, especially in the early years, which only added to the confusion (mistaken by many for freedom) and economic dislocation. In fact, Cuba's leader faced the same choices open to any small power.

Appearing insignificant was the option least likely to appeal to Castro, for two reasons. First, the revolution itself was never thought of as strictly a local matter. Derived from Martí and Marx, Castro's principles were universalist from the beginning.[18] Second, its geographical location made it virtually impossible for Cuba to carry out a radical, anti-American revolution and still appear strategically insignificant. The variant of unimportance is neutrality. There is some evidence that the regime considered this,[19] but it was never adopted as a carefully stated policy. Again, there was the problem of being too close to the United States and not being strategically irrelevant.

That left two possible policies, which had the virtue of not being mutually exclusive. Cuban representatives in the OAS and the United Nations asserted their country's sovereignty and equality. Since its exclusion from the OAS in 1961, Cuba has been extremely active in a long list of international organizations, a number of which it founded.[20] In recent years the regime has enthusiastically supported Latin American organizations which have grown up outside of the OAS and which are attended by government officials, not guerrillas.[21]

But for a small power such demands, even when reinforced by voting victories, do not provide sufficient security. The search for an ally was inevitable if Cuba were to continue to act in the classic fashion of the small power at bay. The search could not have been very long. Quite aside from ideological predilections, the Soviet Union seems, in retrospect, to have been the only serious potential ally for Cuba. The Soviet Union alone could match the neighboring giant and had few interests that would conflict with an anti-American alliance. Moreover, while not as remote as China, the Soviet Union was not overwhelmingly close, and the two countries were beginning

---

[18] There is, of course, the strong possibility that Castro's self-esteem made the insignificance option unlikely. As Hugh Thomas quite rightly pointed out in the spring of 1959: "No Cuban had been so famous as Castro. Already shepherds in Spain and wool workers in Yorkshire had heard of 'Fidel'; and he, a keen student of the international press, knew that they knew." Thomas, *Cuba*, p. 1,195.

[19] Ibid., p. 1,088.

[20] The January 1966 Tricontinental Congress and its offshoot, the Latin American Solidarity Organization (LASO), come to mind.

[21] Nor does the United States belong to these organizations, for that matter. They include OLADE, the Latin American Energy Organization.

to share a similar world view.[22] There remained the danger of becoming a Soviet satellite. Until 1968, Castro took great pains to preserve an independent position on a number of issues including the Sino-Soviet dispute and the proper revolutionary path in Latin America. But since that time, Cuba has moved much closer to the Russian viewpoint, and areas of divergence are few and rarely exposed in public. The reason for this change is undoubtedly Cuba's growing dependence on the Russians for economic and technical assistance, especially after the 1970 ten-million-ton sugar production fiasco.[23] In addition to becoming a satellite, there are other dangers in an unequal alliance. These seem especially relevant to current Soviet-American-Cuban relations and will be discussed below.[24]

It is already clear that on one level Cuba has acted in classical small-power fashion. It has also, it might be added, followed the advice of Belgium's King Albert in maintaining a formidable army of its own.[25] Such patterns are not likely to be altered through conventional diplomacy or even solemn public guarantees of nonintervention.

Castro and the United States

As if Cuba's past, its nationalism, and the peculiar problems of the small power were not obstacles enough to improved relations between the United States and Cuba, there is the character of those relations since 1959. Our purpose here is not to chronicle the facts and controversies of the recent past[26] or to fix blame for the current impasse.

---

[22] Has Castro considered the possibility of a small-power alliance? The answer is probably a qualified "yes." In the late 1960s he seemed to be forging close ties with the North Vietnamese and North Korean regimes. It is obvious that an alliance of three small Communist states was not intended to be a substitute for alliance with the Soviet Union. More likely Castro hoped that the militantly anti-American three would act as a pressure group on the Soviet Union which was giving its first indications of seeking détente with the U.S. Recently enthusiasm for this small power entente has seemed to wane in Cuba. It has been replaced by a resumption of good relations with a select list of Latin American states.

[23] The desperate energy with which this campaign was pursued was often rationalized in terms of anti-Americanism and anti-imperialism. But it is likely that the effort served another purpose, namely, to somehow shorten the time of dependency on the Soviet Union. The latter had already demonstrated its power over the Cubans by slowing down oil shipments to Cuba in 1967.

[24] See below, Chapter 5, pp. 76-81.

[25] Rothstein, *Alliances*, p. 95.

[26] The best accounts are found in Draper, *Castroism, Theory and Practice;* Suárez, *Castroism and Communism;* K. S. Karol, *Guerrillas in Power,* trans.

One could review the evidence to demonstrate that either side was at fault.[27] But to do so here would be to divert attention from the most important questions: Why were relations so bad, and how does this affect the present attempt at renewing relations?

The Cuban side of the relationship will be examined first. A dramatic break with the United States in 1959, although not inevitable, was certainly probable. The accumulation of problems and resentments, some real, some exaggerated, some imagined, was all that a firebrand like Castro needed. Fidel Castro, thirty-two years old in 1959, was, if nothing else, the prototypical radical nationalist, nurtured on the writings of Martí and the examples of the heroes of the Ten Years' War, the War of Independence, and the anti-Machado movement.

His political beginnings as a law student at the University of Havana in the mid-1940s were distinctly nonideological. Castro joined one of many "action groups" loosely attached to the political parties of the time, but action meant, in fact, unrestricted gang warfare unrelated to ideas and ideals. The men of action, according to one Cuban political scientist, were "of an anarchic, semiliterate, and violent character," in direct contrast to the Communists who emphasized "discipline, were arrogantly doctrinaire, and generally displayed exemplary submissiveness."[28] By 1950, however, Castro had moved beyond this level of political involvement and had become active in the *Partido del Pueblo Cubano*, better known as the *Ortodoxos*, who, until the formation of Castro's own 26th of July Movement, embraced the most extreme form of Cuban nationalism.

Castro made remarkably few public statements regarding the United States before 1959, and at least one of those he did make was plainly deceptive.[29] Privately, he wrote to fellow militant Celia Sán-

---

Arnold Pomerans (New York: Hill and Wang, 1970); for an inside official American account, see Philip W. Bonsal, *Cuba, Castro, and the United States* (Pittsburgh: University of Pittsburgh Press, 1971). Bonsal was the U.S. ambassador to Cuba from 1959 until the break in relations in July 1960.

[27] The best evidence suggests that Castro was anxious at a very early stage to break with the United States and that he exaggerated or even manufactured issues to accomplish this end. Castro's hypersensitivity to U.S. press criticism of the early trials is an example of the former, his denunciation of "U.S. aggression" after the Díaz Lanz pamphletting of Havana by air, an example of the latter. Thomas, *Cuba*, pp. 1,075-76 and pp. 1,245-46. Also Draper, *Castroism, Theory and Practice*, p. 122, and especially Bonsal, *Cuba, Castro, and the United States*, pp. 104-7.

[28] Suárez, *Castroism and Communism*, p. 15.

[29] In an article printed in *Coronet*, February 1958, Castro denied he had "any secret plans in my pocket for seizing all foreign holdings." He openly withdrew the earlier program of nationalization of U.S.-owned utilities, finding national-

chez in early June 1958: "When this war is over, a much longer and more important war will begin for me, the war I shall have to wage against the Americans. I feel that this is my destiny."[30] After he came to power, Castro expressed his resentment of the United States more frequently and publicly. Indeed, his first speech after Batista's flight contained one reference to the United States as the unwelcome guest ally in Cuba's war of independence.[31]

The desire to break from the past, especially from Cuba's dependence on America, was very much on his mind when Castro received an invitation from the American Society of Newspaper Editors the following month. Although it was no official invitation, and despite the advice of men like National Bank director Felipe Pazos, Castro seemed doubtful. "But suppose Eisenhower invites me to the White House?" he is reported to have asked. Clearly the young revolutionary was afraid of any early association with the American government. This attitude was apparent, too, at his first press conference on the Washington visit. Castro declared that foreign aid was not being sought: "No, we are proud to be independent and we have no intention of asking anyone for anything."[32]

The preoccupation with the past is even more obvious in Castro's treatment of the new American ambassador to Havana, Philip W.

---

ization "at best, a cumbersome instrument." Quoted from "Why We Fight," *Coronet*, February 1958, and reprinted in Rolando E. Bonachea and Nelson P. Valdés, eds., *Revolutionary Struggle: The Selected Writings of Fidel Castro* (Cambridge: MIT Press, 1972), vol. 1, pp. 364-67. Earlier in his famous *History Will Absolve Me* pamphlet, "he made no major attack on the U.S.—indeed, Castro spoke less violently of the 'colossus of the north' than most Cuban nationalist politicians of the previous fifty years. . . ." Thomas, *Cuba*, p. 851. The full text is in Bonachea and Valdés, eds., *Revolutionary Struggle*, pp. 164-221.

[30] The quote appears in part in Karol, *Guerrillas in Power*, p. 178, and in its entirety in Bonachea and Valdés, eds., *Revolutionary Struggle*, p. 379. The letter was not made public until 27 August 1967 in *Granma Weekly Review* (Havana), p. 8.

[31] Castro was not alone in this resentment. Cuban nationalists for years campaigned against the term *La Guerra Hispano-Americana* until the Cuban congress passed a law in May 1945 making it *La Guerra Hispano-Cubanoamericana*. Duvon C. Corbitt, "Cuban Revisionist Interpretations of Cuba's Struggle for Independence," *Hispanic-American Historical Review*, vol. 43 (August 1963), p. 402.

[32] Quoted in Thomas, *Cuba*, pp. 1,199-2,000, 1,209. Thirteen days earlier, Castro had told a Cuban television audience that he was considering loan requests to the World Bank and the Export-Import Bank. Ibid., p. 1,209. The highest-ranking American official he met, of course, was then Vice President Nixon. Castro said little of this encounter; his longest statement appeared in *Hoy*, 16 March 1959, p. 4. *Hoy* was the daily of the *Partido Socialista Popular*, Cuba's Communist party. Castro's statement on Nixon was not critical. See Thomas, *Cuba*, p. 1,211, footnote 61.

Bonsal. Bonsal was a career diplomat with experience in Latin America (including Cuba)[33] and was well known for his sympathy with all revolutionary movements which threw out old-style military dictators. Bonsal's intentions were liberal and he was sensitive to Cuban feelings.[34] He would write later:

> During my first weeks in Havana I endeavored through as many channels as possible to convey goodwill and a readiness to enter into serious negotiations *on any matters* the regime might wish to raise. I took the unusual step of making publicized calls on each of the ministers in Castro's Cabinet. I tried to develop with each one of them a relationship of cordial confidence and to instill in them a belief that the government of the United States was prepared to give the most sympathetic and constructive consideration to any proposals of the new Cuban government in the field of relations between the two countries. I emphasized . . . the elements of mutual and reciprocal advantage inherent in the existing relationship between Cuba and the United States. I made every effort to avoid the attitude of thinly disguised paternalism which these people had been taught to believe had characterized some of my predecessors.[35]

Besides these goodwill gestures there were specific measures, largely economic, that the U.S. government was prepared to discuss. They included: a new Cuban tariff structure that would stimulate industrialization and agricultural diversification; a formula permitting Cuban nationalization of some American property including the utilities and sugar cane land—without discouraging further U.S. private investment; and short-term assistance to bail out Cuba's finances which were in terrible shape thanks to Batista's mismanagement and plain looting of the treasury. In addition, it was the ambassador's private hope that the Guantánamo agreement could also be modified to include Cuban involvement in the operation of the base.[36]

Bonsal was attempting to establish what later policy makers would call a mature partnership. The worst that could be said for

---

[33] Bonsal had spent several months in Cuba in 1926 as a trainee with the ITT subsidiary, the Cuban Telephone Company, and in 1938-1939 was vice-consul and third secretary at the embassy, and Cuban desk officer the following year. Bonsal, *Cuba, Castro, and the United States*, pp. 26-27.

[34] Bonsal arrived in Havana on the evening of 19 February 1959; Castro not only did not meet the new ambassador, he took the opportunity to give the most anti-American speech of his career. Ibid., p. 38.

[35] Ibid., p. 51. The emphasis is mine.

[36] Ibid., pp. 40-42.

it was that the attempt to change the traditional relationship had come too late. Moreover, Bonsal's initiative had strong State Department backing from William Wieland, chief of the Caribbean office, and the assistant secretary of state for Latin American affairs, Roy Rubottom. Early critics of the Castro regime like former Ambassador to Cuba Earl Smith and Ambassador Whiting Willauer (Costa Rica) were not directly responsible for making the Cuban policy.[37]

Eagerness to please, however, netted Bonsal and the United States very little. In the first place, despite Bonsal's best efforts, Castro avoided discussing anything seriously with the ambassador for nearly four months—a dramatic reversal of the traditional relationship.[38] The reason was rooted in Fidel Castro's views of Cuban history. Once before, he believed, a revolutionary regime had overthrown a dictator, and once before a new American ambassador, professing friendship, had undermined the regime and replaced it with a dependable ally, Fulgencio Batista. Castro feared that his 1959 revolution would be a repetition of 1933 and that Bonsal would prove to be another Sumner Welles.[39] Young and unsure of himself, Fidel Castro was determined not to be another Grau San Martín. It is no wonder that he would later speak of Bonsal as acting and being treated like a proconsul.[40]

The fear of repeating history was only a small part of what went wrong.[41] Other factors, less easy to document perhaps, were of great importance. Thus, while Fidel Castro may have felt insecure in dealing with the northern colossus, his own ambition helped the unravelling of U.S.-Cuban ties. If there were one valid conclusion that Fidel Castro could draw from Cuba's history, it was his country's

---

37 Thomas, *Cuba*, pp. 1,206-7.

38 Bonsal, *Cuba, Castro, and the United States*, pp. 73-74. This is not to suggest that Bonsal was unable to establish contact with members of the Cuban government. He did, especially with Castro's first foreign minister, Roberto Agramonte.

39 Castro was seven when these events occurred.

40 Bonsal, *Cuba, Castro and the United States*, p. 91; Thomas, *Cuba*, p. 1,200 and footnote 27. For the complete text of Castro's lengthiest criticism of Bonsal's behavior, see Lee Lockwood, *Castro's Cuba, Cuba's Fidel: An American Journalist's Inside Look at Today's Cuba* (New York: Macmillan Co., 1967), p. 141.

41 Already by September 1960 Castro's feelings about the United States were being colored by non-Cuban events. He told K. S. Karol at that time: "Cuba's case is almost identical with that of the Congo and Algeria. We want our independence and the North Americans reply by waging the most perfidious war against us, trying to bring further ruin on a country they have been systematically bleeding for more than half a century. But they won't get away with it. Sooner or later, the American people will come to realize what injustices they are inflicting on Cuba." Quoted in Karol, *Guerrillas in Power*, p. 8.

lack of a great man—a founder of a permanent political and social order. The hero José Martí, great writer and practitioner of exile politics, did not live long enough to play that role. And Cuba's great revolutionaries, Céspedes, Gómez, and Maceo, are acknowledged even by their admirers to have been fighters, not founders.

Castro's opportunity then was unique, a fact that hardly escaped him. It was also one he would not share—especially with a newly indulgent America trying to pull Cuba out of its miserable past. Castro's radical rejection of America's traditional role was a decision warmly encouraged by his closest advisers who were young, radical, and had shared the life of the Sierra.[42] The older and more moderate men in Castro's first government, like Agramonte and Pazos, did not and could not have the same influence as Castro's battlefield comrades. Nor did younger but less radical men like Ernesto Betancourt (also not in the Sierra) have any greater success. In retrospect, all that the liberals accomplished was delay, acting as buffers between the radicals who were in control and the Americans.

Castro's Conversion to Communism. This partial explanation for Castro's policy toward the United States during the early part of the revolution still leaves unexplained the conversion to Marxism which Castro so dramatically announced in public on 1 December 1961.[43] Why did he do it, and what does it mean for the future course of Cuban-American relations?

The switch to Soviet-style Marxism could not have been easy for Castro, for personal and political reasons. The action group he had joined as a young man and the leftist *Ortodoxo* party to which he had subsequently belonged were both anti-Communist. Their anticommunism, however, was not rooted in the cold war. Cubans tended to be anti-Communist out of opposition to the *Partido Socialista Popular* (PSP), an orthodox, pro-Soviet Communist party which had collaborated with Batista in the 1940s and had refused to endorse

---

[42] The inner circle included his brother Raul, Ernesto Guevara, Carlos Rafael Rodrígues, and perhaps Raul Castro's wife, Vilma Espín. With the exception of Guevara, they remain sixteen years later at the center of the circle. Raul Castro had been a member of the Cuban Communist party's (PSP) youth organization in the early 1950s. Carlos Rafael Rodrígues, an older man, was a member of the PSP and had served in Batista's cabinet. The survival of the Talleyrand of the Cuban revolution was not due to his PSP credentials, but to his early conversion to the Castro cause. Thomas, *Cuba*, p. 826, and Suárez, *Castroism and Communism*, p. 57.

[43] The best account is in Suárez, *Castroism and Communism*, especially pp. 70-153.

armed struggle against the dictator after he seized power again in March 1952.[44]

Not only Castro but many of his followers were prejudiced against Cuban Communists. It is not surprising, then, that Castro continued to criticize the Communists for more than six months *after* the flight of Batista. Even then his shift in position was carefully qualified—nothing that would deeply offend his anti-Communist supporters: "Our position in regard to this problem of the Communists is very clear. . . . It is that in my opinion it is hardly honorable for us to start campaigns and attacks against them just in order to prevent people from accusing us of being Communists ourselves."[45]

It is sometimes argued that this small peace offering (which the PSP seized eagerly) and others that followed were meant to forge an alliance between the Communists and the *fidelistas* because of Castro's desperate need for a program and cadres to administer it. There is some evidence to sustain this argument. First, it is true that Castro lacked any coherent, workable program; he certainly had no plan that would pull Cuba out of its financial woes and bring about rapid economic development. Moreover, even if such a program had existed, Castro lacked men who were loyal to him *and* were capable of running the machinery of government and industry.

Nevertheless, this argument can do no more than demonstrate need. Castro, in fact, ignored the rather cautious programs produced by the PSP leadership [46] and plunged ahead with a series of "reforms" that would leave the Communists panting to catch up and the economy in a shambles. Nor did the PSP contribute much in the way of cadres. Few were given responsible positions of any sort—nor was their merit as administrators ever established. And most important, Castro's use of the PSP did not oblige him in any way to become a Communist, any more than it had obliged Batista to do so in the 1940s. The PSP had found it ideologically acceptable to work with Batista and could have devised a formula for dealing with an old-fashioned "putchist" like Castro without taxing in the slightest the ideological wizardry of Blas Roca, Aníbal Escalante, and Carlos Rafael

---

[44] The most detailed picture of the PSP's unpopularity is drawn by Karol, *Guerrillas in Power*, pp. 81-186. The PSP's single greatest error in dealing with Castro was its criticism of his attack on the Moncada barracks as "putchist." The issue is still a sensitive one as demonstrated by Castro's retelling the story during the 1974 26 July speech.

[45] Quoted in Suárez, *Castroism and Communism*, p. 55.

[46] See the PSP's "The Overthrow of the Tyranny and the Immediate Tasks Ahead," published in *Hoy*, 6 January 1959 (the day of Castro's arrival in Havana) and analyzed in Suárez, *Castroism and Communism*, pp. 38-43.

Rodrígues. Castro owed them nothing—least of all a confession of faith.[47]

But if the PSP was not needed for these reasons, perhaps Castro saw in them the kind of disciplined force he needed to help keep him in power.[48] The *Líder Máximo* maintained his power in the early days by frequent contact with the masses via radio and television— by sheer charismatic appeal, puzzling to some observers. At that time he had no police, no real army,[49] and no party; the 26th of July Movement, never very well organized, fell apart early in 1959.[50] But Castro had survived in the snake pit of Cuban politics long enough to know he must be careful. Rhetoric alone would not keep him on top forever. He had a following and he had created great expectations among the poor and near poor, especially in the capital, but the appeal of income redistribution would last only as long as there were goods to hand out. The problem was compounded by the fact that much of the loot belonged to North Americans, and seizure of that property would involve conflict with the United States. Thus, Castro's real problem was how to remain in power after committing Cuba to a radical social revolution. Allying himself with the PSP was in itself of little help, but it served a purpose as a signal to the Soviet Union.

The need for Soviet economic or even military aid was not a sufficient condition for Castro's adopting Marxism-Leninism. Others like Sukarno or Nasser had cooperated with the Soviet Union without doing so. But they did not have his special problem: a neighboring,

---

[47] Even after Castro's conversion, the PSP has not fared well. First, Aníbal Escalante was disgraced in 1962. In 1964 the young PSP informer, Marcos Rodrígues, was put on trial for betraying Havana revolutionaries to the Batista police. In 1967 a so-called "microfaction" consisting of old PSP cadres headed by the unfortunate Escalante were discovered and punished. Lesser humiliations have been visited on Blas Roca and Juan Marinello. See Suárez, *Castroism and Communism*, pp. 146-52, 201-9; Thomas, *Cuba*, pp. 1,468-69.

[48] K. S. Karol has refined the conventional argument on this point by seeing the "headlong rush into nationalization" without trained administrators as forcing Castro to draw on anyone with discipline and organizational skills which, he says, the Cuban leader thought important at the time. He adds, "[The Communists] were also advocates of a hierarchical power structure, in which socialist ideas and plans are dispensed to the people from above, and were accustomed to taking the sagacity of their leaders for granted." But even granting this, using the PSP did not force him to adopt their world view. Karol, *Guerrillas in Power*, p. 185.

[49] Suárez estimates that the total size of the rebel army *after* Batista fled was 1,500 men, including perhaps only 300 reliable old-timers. Suárez, *Castroism and Communism*, p. 33.

[50] At its height the 26th of July Movement numbered fewer than 400 in Havana. Ibid., p. 33.

threatening superpower. Even more important, the Cuban premier wanted far more than agreements to buy sugar[51] and a cheap, plentiful supply of weapons. Castro needed a firm Soviet pledge to defend the island, which was precisely what other recipients of Russian aid outside the Warsaw bloc had never gotten or probably even requested. To extract that promise Castro had to do more than profess friendship for the great Soviet people, as the Nassers had done. He must become a bona fide member of the faith.

But the Russians had reservations. Like many well trained members of an orthodox priesthood, the Soviet leaders were skeptical of miracles. Maybe in the old days of Lenin. . . . But the fact was that no regime had become Marxist-Leninist without the help of the Red Army, or at least a long period of popular front "democratic rule" during which the local Communists gradually assumed total power.[52] Therefore, Castro's diatribes against America (welcome to the Soviet leaders, but hardly unknown in Latin America) were not enough for the Kremlin. Nor was his declaration, made immediately after the Bay of Pigs victory, that the Cuban revolution was indeed a socialist one sufficient. The world, after all, was full of socialists—even the Trotskyites dared to be that. Such an avowal was in itself quite worthless. Even Castro's remarkable 1 December profession of faith did not move the Russians immediately.[53] It was only five months later that they acknowledged for the first time in a May Day slogan

---

[51] President Eisenhower cut the Cuban sugar quota to zero on 16 December 1960. Karol, *Guerrillas in Power*, p. 118.

[52] Other observers have stressed that Soviet hesitation in accepting Cuba was also due to Khrushchev's earnest pursuit of détente with Eisenhower until the May 1960 U-2 incident and the prudent concern arising from the fact that Cuba, after all, did lie within the American sphere of influence.

[53] The Russians, of course, were not completely aloof. They signed a trade agreement in February 1960 and sent arms (via Czechoslovakia) five months later. In that same month (July), Khrushchev, in the wake of the U-2 affair and the cancelled summit meeting in Paris, declared, "In a figurative sense, if it became necessary, the Soviet military can support the Cuban people with rocket weapons. . . ." Quoted in Suárez, *Castroism and Communism*, p. 93. Much to the Soviet premier's embarrassment, Castro seized on this "offer" and reassured the Cuban people that real, not figurative, rockets were ready to fly on behalf of the Cuban revolution. Meanwhile, Khrushchev swiftly retreated, using a communiqué issued jointly by him and Raul Castro as a way out. No mention was made of the rockets. Suárez, *Castro and Communism*, pp. 93-94. Even in September, Khrushchev was still backpedalling. In answer to a question from an American journalist as to whether the rocket pledge were true, he replied: "More or less true. . . . You need not worry. . . . Since America is not going to attack Cuba, there can be no danger." Quoted in Michel Tatu, *Power in the Kremlin: From Khrushchev to Kosygin*, trans. Helen Katel (New York: Viking Press, 1968), p. 231.

that the "heroic people of Cuba" were "embarked on the path of building socialism."[54]

American Policy toward Cuba

The Shaky Foundations of American Policy. America's Cuban policy in the early years of the Castro regime was marked by confusion and uncertainty. Its climax was the Bay of Pigs operation which Theodore Draper has so rightly called "one of those rare politico-military events—a perfect failure";[55] so great a failure, in fact, that (as Draper also rightly observed) it paralyzed American policy for over a year.[56]

The feebleness of this policy was a result of two factors. First, top policy makers in this country had long ceased taking Cuba seriously. The last first-rate diplomat to be involved with Cuba was Sumner Welles. In the nuclear age it was unthinkable that the United States could be challenged on its doorstep. The geopolitical concerns of Jefferson, Adams, and Mahan had vanished.[57] It is not surprising

---

[54] *Pravda*, 15 April 1962, p. 1, reprinted in *Current Digest of the Soviet Press*, 9 May 1962, pp. 9-12. The slogan on Cuba (number 26) followed immediately the one devoted to Czechoslovakia (an orthodox police state) and preceded the slogan on Yugoslavia (a heterodox Communist state at best, but one with which the Soviet Union had good relations in 1962). More important, Cuba ranked well above such third world nations as Algeria, India, and Indonesia. Moreover, the editor of *Pravda* extended "fraternal greetings" to the Cubans while only giving "warm greetings" to the Indians et al. The full text of this benchmark slogan reads: "Fraternal greetings to the heroic people of Cuba, who have embarked on the path of building socialism and are selflessly defending the freedom and independence of their homeland! May the friendship and cooperation between the peoples of the Soviet Union and Cuba develop and grow stronger."

[55] Theodore Draper, *Castro's Revolution: Myths and Realities* (New York: Praeger, 1962), p. 59. Along with their other oversights, the architects of Playa Girón were probably unaware of the long list of failed expeditionary landings to liberate Cuba that occurred in the nineteenth century.

[56] Draper, *Castroism, Theory and Practice*, p. 135.

[57] See, for example, Dexter Perkins's confident judgment made in 1947: "Suppose, for example, a full-fledged Communist regime should some day be established in Cuba, a regime which definitely asserted its acceptance of the Communist faith, and which formed close relations with the U.S.S.R. . . . Could the United States stand idly by, and watch the establishment in the New World, and not so far from its own shores, of a government whose principles it detested, and whose practical policies it could not fail to oppose?

"No doubt in such circumstances there would be those who would not wish to press the principle of nonintervention to this, its absolute conclusion. A thoroughly Communist regime in Cuba would, in practice, not only involve American property interests to a very substantial degree, but it would also present a very definite threat to the security of the United States itself. It might well be used as a center for espionage in time of peace, and of espionage and sabotage

that by October 1959 an American president could be as baffled as Eisenhower clearly was when asked to comment on Fidel Castro's behavior:

> I have no idea of discussing possible motivations of such a man . . . certainly I am not qualified to go into such an abstruse and difficult subject as that . . . here after all is a country that you believe, on the basis of our history, would be one of our real friends. . . . It would seem to be a puzzling matter to figure just exactly why the Cubans would not be, and the Cuban Government would be, so unhappy when, after all, their principal market is right here. . . .[58]

Second, some serious misconceptions were widespread among policy makers. One of these was articulated by Ambassador Bonsal himself. On his arrival in Havana he felt

> that the Cuban establishment, including the politicians who had opposed Batista and those citizens (from "capitalists" through "the emerging middle class" to the members of the labor unions) who had enjoyed relative economic stability and security, now had a major role to play. This establishment would, I thought, confine the new government and the leaders from the Sierra Maestre, including Castro, within democratic patterns of behavior. Thus a national program of renewal and progress would eventually be agreed upon and implemented through an orderly political mechanism with roots in the Cuban past.[59]

This passage is quoted *in extenso* because it embodies a number of fallacies which the U.S. liberal community holds about "political development" in general and Cuban politics in particular. It assumes, in the first place, that political change is linear and in the direction of decency and democracy. That history has not headed that way for some time should be apparent by now. Indeed, it should have been in 1959. Second, it is difficult to understand why it was thought that the middle class in Cuba would hold Castro in line. That class

---

in time of war. It would undeniably place problems of defense in a new context, and it would provide encouragement for those who seek to undermine the Pan-American solidarity which is, or at any rate ought to be, one of the objectives of American policy." Dexter Perkins, *The United States and the Caribbean* (Cambridge: Harvard University Press, 1947), pp. 159-60.

[58] Quoted in Thomas, *Cuba*, pp. 1,248-49. I do not wish to make too much of Eisenhower's confusion. After all, he was honest in his bewilderment, while experts continued to reach erroneous conclusions about the Cuban revolution. Nevertheless, for an American president to be so poorly briefed on a matter that earlier presidents had thought vital is striking.

[59] Bonsal, *Cuba, Castro, and the United States*, pp. 4-5.

had never succeeded in holding any leader to account until his rule had become so onerous that small groups of desperate men began to act. Moreover, even those activists sometimes found it easier to leave—a comfortable exile was always possible in the United States and certainly preferable to a painful death.

The proximity of this country offered another kind of escape from responsibility to genuinely decent and politically active Cubans: the United States, they assumed, would never accept a Communist regime. As an exile later explained to Bonsal: "We had no confidence in any possible Cuban leadership of the anti-Castro forces, and we did not believe that you, the United States, would let Castro get away with it."[60]

Even more important is the nature of the Cuban middle class: it is an old mistake to think of the "emerging Latin American middle class" as similar to its American and European counterparts. The fact is it is not. Latin middle classes are more heterogeneous in their political values, and they do not share our political habits. This was especially true for the Cuban middle class which had remained insecure during the Spanish regime by being excluded from nearly all normal middle-class pursuits except the professions and politics. It had never been a buffer against extremism. More often it had been a promotor of revolution[61] since its own aspirations were being steadily thwarted.[62] Finally, the Cuban middle class proved unable to check Castro's extremism not because observers like Bonsal misjudged the power of Fidel Castro. People awash in sociological generalizations tend to forget that leaders like Castro are not stopped by faceless entities like the "middle class"; they are stopped by other people. But no one had Castro's extraordinary prestige and ability to attract a fanatical following. Furthermore, Castro had unleashed a flood of expectations from Havana's lower class, especially its unorganized masses—the despised lumpenproletariat of Marx. Anyone challenging Fidel Castro risked being torn apart by the mob, and sophisticated Cubans knew this.

---

[60] Ibid., p. 6.

[61] Antonio Guiteras, José Antonio Mella, the Castro brothers, and much of the 26th of July leadership were solidly middle class in origin. One of the few Cuban leaders in recent years who did not come from the middle class was Fulgencio Batista, a sugar worker's son from northeast Cuba. Thomas, *Cuba*, pp. 635-36.

[62] There is possibly another reason for the Cuban's inability to prevent a recurring pattern of tyranny: namely, the easygoing nature of the Cubans themselves. I have no civic culture data to prove this (no one does), but it is a fact that the resistance movements against Machado, Batista, and Castro have numbered in the few thousands at most and have been dominated by the young.

What is more, Fidel Castro did deliver. There was a radical redistribution of income in the early years of the revolution in favor of the urban marginal poor. They received, for instance, substantial increases in medical and educational benefits that were permanent and boosts in disposable income that proved more ephemeral as the regression of the economy brought about the "ration state." Nevertheless, these improvements created an unshakable loyalty to the regime from a large number of Cubans who had hardly been part of the nation under the previous regime. Castro's social changes did help to mold a people, albeit by means of a principle (confiscation of other people's wealth) less lofty than his apologists would like to have it.

American assessments of the political resilience of Cuban society were exaggerated. And so was the belief that a commitment to a specific set of reforms was sufficiently widespread among Cubans that, if these were not instituted, the Castro regime would be brought to a speedy end. In fact, there was no such program, only a widespread hope that things would be better now that the tyrant had fled. Beyond that, Castro had nearly a clean slate to write on.

American confusion was also a result of raging controversy within the administration since not everyone was as puzzled as the president.[63] On the one hand, men like Rubottom and Bonsal were convinced that Castro was not a Communist. Others, like Ambassador Robert Hill and ex-ambassador Earl Smith, stoutly maintained that he was, or at best perilously close to it. Supporting the first view (which predominated for at least a year in Washington) was the CIA. General Charles Cabell, deputy director of the agency, stated in Senate testimony in early November 1959 that:

> Castro is not a Communist . . . the Cuban Communists do not consider him a Communist party member or even pro-Communist. . . . It is questionable whether the Communists desire to recruit Castro into the Communist party, that they could do so if they wished or that he would be susceptible to Communist discipline if he joined.[64]

---

[63] Vice President Nixon after his first meeting with Castro in May 1959 is reported to have remarked that the Cuban premier was either the most naive man he had ever met or he was a Communist. Mr. Nixon, however, has never indicated which explanation he personally favored. See Thomas, *Cuba*, p. 1,210. Also Richard M. Nixon, *Six Crises* (New York: Doubleday and Co., 1962), pp. 351-52.

[64] U.S. Congress, Senate, Hearings of the Internal Security Subcommittee, *Communist Threat to the U.S.A. through the Caribbean*, 1959-1962, and quoted in Thomas, *Cuba*, p. 1,249. For the internal debate, see Thomas, *Cuba*, pp. 1,206-8. It is true that those who suspected Castro of being a Communist had not proved

Patience, Firmness, and Countermeasures. In the midst of this tangle of misperceptions and internal debate, the government's watchwords were patience and firmness. To conservative critics there was not nearly enough firmness, while liberals felt patience too often was lacking.[65] In fact, the watchwords were only a cover for a series of ad hoc measures planned and executed after any number of Castro initiatives.

At first, U.S. strategy was shaped by our embassy, which attempted to win favor by ignoring Castro's more provocative actions. It was a policy of fighting fire with water. For example, in March 1959, when the American-owned Cuban telephone company was taken over and rates reduced with no compensation offered, the ambassador chose to ignore the incident as such, except to offer the Cuban ministry of communications technical assistance on telephone rate regulation.[66] In regard to land reform, which often amounted to mere aimless, violent, and illegal seizure of property, the United States expressed sympathy for the concept and "emphasized the goodwill and the desire for accommodation of the United States in the face of the situations arising from the new state of affairs in Cuba."[67] After Castro heatedly denounced the United States for "intervention" in the wake of the Díaz Lanz "bombing" (charges he knew were not true), Assistant Secretary Rubottom gave out assurances of nonintervention on 26 October 1959, which were followed by a similar statement issued by Ambassador Bonsal.[68]

Patience and understanding failed to stop Fidel Castro from radicalizing the revolution. At best our low profile made us a more difficult target to hit. After our benign reaction to land reform, for example, Castro announced that the U.S. action had been proper and the American ambassador "cordial and respectful."[69] The new mood, however, did not last through the summer.

---

their case, but the more liberal officials, while correct about Castro's relations with the PSP, were too committed to the belief that Castro could only be a social reformer. They did not or would not see Castro for what he was: a radical of Jacobin instincts with no experience or commitment to democratic procedure or civil liberties.

[65] The liberals could point to economic sanctions like cutting the sugar quota and the conservatives could argue that the irregular, often illegal, seizure of American property under the guise of land reform was met by a wholly inadequate U.S. response.

[66] Bonsal, *Cuba, Castro, and the United States*, pp. 46-48.

[67] Ibid., p. 74.

[68] Ibid., p. 113.

[69] Ibid., p. 74. Bonsal records Castro's comment to Herbert Matthews that "the American reaction to the agrarian reform of May 1959 made me realize that there was no chance of an accommodation with the United States." Ibid., p. 75.

Firmness succeeded patience in early 1960 but with no better success, perhaps less. If patience had been water on fire, firmness was a blast of pure oxygen. Further major attacks on U.S. interests would be met with some kind of retaliatory action. The first, taken secretly in March 1960, was Eisenhower's authorization of the training of Cuban exiles—an order that would culminate fourteen months later in the Bay of Pigs disaster.[70] Overt responses followed within a few months. Quite probably in reaction to Castro's vehement verbal attack on the United States after the explosion of a French munitions ship in Havana harbor, Washington advised American-owned refineries not to process Soviet crude oil. Castro's reaction was simple: the refineries were nationalized. In turn, the United States suspended the balance of Cuba's sugar quota for the second half of 1960.[71] The fatal downward spiral had begun and would end in the rupture of relations in January 1961—with Fidel Castro quite typically taking the initiative. The Cuban premier ordered the American embassy to cut its staff to an impossibly low number, and the United States, faced with this humiliating ultimatum, broke off diplomatic relations.

Firmness, then, netted this country very little. Even worse, it suited Castro's purposes admirably. He did need an enemy to consolidate his position, but one that could not, or would not, actually destroy him. In the meantime, the limited American response let the Cuban regime move at its own pace toward some arrangement with the Soviet bloc.

Finally, I would argue, the Bay of Pigs operation was a distillation of the American style in firmness. It was a limited attempt to overthrow an already well-entrenched regime by an extremely difficult military operation, the amphibious assault. Like other firm American actions, it again "proved" U.S. hostility without actually endangering the Castro regime. Moreover, it provided Castro with a splendid opportunity to wipe out the remaining opposition and thus pushed Cuba further along the road to police-state socialism.

Would anything else have worked? Powerful forces were driving these countries apart. It can be argued that no American policy could have prevented the Castro government from becoming hostile. Perhaps this was so. But another approach could hardly have brought

---

[70] This decision is sometimes anachronistically taken as a decision to invade Cuba relatively early in the course of the revolution. In fact, Eisenhower approved a contingency force of Cuban exiles which at an unspecified date could be introduced surreptitiously into the island in order to carry out guerrilla activities and eventually destroy the regime. Neither Eisenhower nor the CIA planners realized the extent to which they were repeating history.

[71] Bonsal, *Cuba, Castro, and the United States*, pp. 151-53.

worse results. The following proposed course of action has relevance for policy makers today.

What is clear is that the United States had forgotten that the Caribbean was vital to this country. Since World War II at least, we had treated it as a backwater: our interests in the area were not clearly defined, nor was a course of action commensurate with those interests spelled out. Facing a new, radical, and still unsettled regime in Havana, the United States failed to lay out at an early date, in a highly confidential manner and in clear, unmistakable terms, what political developments in Cuba would be acceptable to this country. A Communist regime supported by the Soviet Union would not be and, in fact, would invite military action. A radical nationalist government that confiscated American property without compensation would not be attacked but could expect no help from us, not even a sugar quota. A moderate nationalist regime could receive our warm support, including short-term aid. Negotiations with such a regime might proceed over a wide range of matters, from the rules on American investment to Guantánamo.[72]

This approach would have presented Fidel Castro with a range of choices, each with predictable results, instead of a guessing game about U.S. intentions. Generous but firm limits spelled out soon after Castro's seizure of power, rather than a period of patient passivity followed by uncoordinated ad hoc countermeasures, should have been our policy. Faced with this range of possibilities, Fidel Castro may well have wavered between extreme and moderate nationalism, but his conversion to communism would have been very unlikely.

Some, of course, find it objectionable that the United States should lay down the law for others in such a "high handed fashion." This is a sensitive matter, but the vital consideration is this: states are not equal and the notion that they are is a polite fiction; and the states that are powerful use their power to protect their interests. This is a truism, but it seems to escape many people. In any case, in the scenario proposed above the United States would not have prevented the Cubans from rearranging their social, political, and economic furniture pretty much as they pleased. Only when they acted in such a way as to threaten our own household would we most rightly have objected.

---

[72] In 1960, the ambassador made a suggestion to State Department officials that the United States persuade the Soviet leaders not to take any "actions that would encourage the Cubans in their aggressive designs on legitimate American interests." This highly useful suggestion was vetoed for reasons not made clear. Ibid., p. 132.

The Policy of Economic Denial, 1964–1974. If the early Castro years were marked by a confused American policy, the decade since the missile crisis has seen a far more mature policy develop. Unfortunately, the zeal of its critics has led them to oversimplify this policy, the more easily to demolish it. Before we move on to a new policy it would be wise to better understand the old.

American policy up until the last few months has been rooted in decisions made more than a decade ago. After the missile crisis, Cuba was not viewed as a direct military threat to either this country or Latin America. The actual threat, it was believed, was indirect, since the Cuban regime was promoting guerrilla-type subversion throughout the region. Subversion was believed to be especially dangerous to "anachronistic societies" which "remain dominated by small elites—tight little oligarchies that control the bulk of the productive wealth."[73] Furthermore, such societies were now, willing or not, undergoing rapid change and experiencing within the space of one or two decades all the convulsions Europe underwent in the nineteenth century. This period of upheaval, American policy makers argued, provided opportunities for the Communists, who were identified as agents of the Soviet Union. Cuba, of course, acted as a convenient springboard, a base for activity in Latin America, a training ground for bolshevism with a Spanish accent.

But Cuba was more than a convenient jump-off point. Its leader had his own personal interest in subversion. At this point, American policy makers agreed on who and what, precisely, Fidel Castro was. In a speech in 1964, Undersecretary of State George Ball said that the Cuban leader thought of himself as a second Simón Bolívar, that is, the liberator of all Latin America. Ball added:

A born revolutionary, driven by a hunger for power and prestige, he looks upon the southern half of the American Continent as a proper field for the fulfillment of his ambitions. He seeks a revolutionary millennium in which the example of Cuba will have swept the continent, and his position of liberator and leader—not of the small island of Cuba, but of all Latin America—will have been assured.[74]

The millennialist ambition of one man would be transmitted to the followers who shared his "psychological and political needs." Both must have their enthusiasm sustained by "the prospect of further advance beyond the confines of the island—an island which they

---

[73] George Ball, "Principles of Our Policy toward Cuba," reprinted in *Department of State Bulletin*, 11 May 1964, p. 738.

[74] Ibid., p. 739.

48

look upon as the base from which the continent-wide revolution will be propagated by word and deed." [75]

After the one-dimensional debate on Castro's political beliefs in the early 1960s, this is a nicely etched psychological portrait. But how should the United States handle a megalomaniac? There are not, it must be admitted, many useful precedents. Nevertheless, in contrast to 1959–1962, the American government did work out a coherent strategy. First, as Secretary Ball indicates, a spectrum of policies had been considered, from direct military action to negotiation. An American invasion would be a direct way to remove the Castro regime, but it would mean war with a small state—and its powerful friend. Blockade was rejected because it too was an act of war. And besides, as Ball was careful to point out, an act of war against Cuba was a policy with no support in this country whatever. At the opposite end of the policy spectrum was negotiation. But negotiation, according to Ball, would only be possible after the elimination of two factors: "First, Castro's political, economic, and military dependence upon the Soviets; and, second, the continuance of Castro's subversive activities in Latin America." [76]

Until these were altered (and Ball specified that we were bound on both points by OAS commitments) talks would remain impossible. Ruling out both war and negotiation (for the moment), the United States was left with a middle course, namely, to operate on two levels. First, Latin American countries must be made invulnerable to subversion in the short run by improving each republic's counterinsurgency capability; in the long run, resistance to "Communist infection" can only be attained through social reform and economic development. [77] Second, in Secretary Ball's words: "we must employ all available instruments of power *less than acts of war* to limit or reduce the ability of the Cuban government to advance the Communist cause in Latin America through propaganda, sabotage, and subversion." [78] In fact, the only available instrument of power less than an act of war was economic denial. With the help of the OAS member states, the United States tried to deny Cuba "those categories of goods that are most vital to the operation of the Cuban economy." [79] In addition, there has been an attempt to cut off free-world shipping

[75] Ibid.
[76] Ibid.
[77] Ibid., pp. 740-41.
[78] Ibid., pp. 739-40. The emphasis is mine.
[79] Ibid., p. 742.

which has forced the Soviet bloc to reallocate its own scarce maritime resources.[80]

The policy of economic denial had four objectives: first, "to reduce the will and ability of the present Cuban regime to export subversion and violence to the other American states";[81] second, to show the Cuban people that the Castro government did not serve their interests—one of which was economic prosperity; third, to demonstrate to Latin Americans that the OAS members would and could collectively resist communism; and finally, to increase the price the Soviet Union would have to pay for the luxury of having a fellow believer in the Caribbean.[82] One objective often ascribed to this policy had in fact been specifically ruled out by George Ball: economic denial, by itself, was thought insufficient to bring down the Castro government. That, of course, was a desirable end, but no policy short of war could bring it about. Thus, by 1964 the United States had tacitly accepted the permanence of the Cuban regime.[83]

Finally, Secretary Ball, again anticipating criticism, defended the policy of economic denial against one Communist state but not against the others. The rationale was simple and, for once, directly pragmatic. Denial caused Cuba a great amount of damage, while it would have caused the Soviet Union, which imported less than 1 percent of its GNP, almost none. The policy of selective economic denial was adopted because it was effective.[84]

This policy, which has endured for ten years, is now under heavy attack. Perhaps no better indication of this is the fact that George Ball, the articulate defender of U.S. Cuban policy in 1964, is an equally articulate critic of it in 1974.[85] What has changed, and how do we go about fashioning a new policy to meet our needs in the Caribbean for the next decade?

---

[80] Ibid.

[81] Ibid., p. 741.

[82] Ibid.

[83] Ibid.

[84] Ibid.

[85] George Ball, "Your Evil Embargo; Our Purity of Purpose," *New York Times*, 22 March 1974. Ball argues that our trade embargo now no longer serves a useful purpose since Cuba is no longer the "center of Communist infection" or "a blueprint for the New Jerusalem." Furthermore, our "misguided efforts to bludgeon other nations into line" will only "poison our relations with Canada and lead to further defections from an obsolete O.A.S. policy."

4
THE NEW WILLINGNESS TO NEGOTIATE

The current debate on Cuba leaves the impression that this problem is somehow left over from the 1960s and that we would do well to settle it, preferably now. This is an oversimplification of course, but basically not far from the truth. Our special nonrelationship with Cuba *is* an anomaly: rarely except in wartime does a nation have so little to do with a neighbor, good or otherwise, for so long. This realization is central to the atmosphere that surrounds the coming negotiations. But when did it emerge and become widespread? How did we get from the George Ball of 1964 to the George Ball of 1974?

The Shift in American Opinion

Events and circumstances have changed, but so have the *perceptions* of events and circumstances discussed by journalists, academics, politicians, and clergymen. To a remarkable degree these influential groups hold similar views, which have had their impact on public opinion. Cuba really became fashionable again with the Nixon administration and has received a great deal of attention in the last two years as détente has become more serious. The beguiling formula—if big Red China, then why not little Red Cuba?—soon became the unexamined wisdom of foreign policy specialists.[1] But the most persistent advocates of policy revision, on this as on other issues, have been members of the American press.

The Press. Both editors and reporters have pressed American officials to admit the failure of the old policy and adopt a new, more realistic

---

[1] This is the curious mirror image of an earlier formula on Cuba: if we fight communism in Vietnam, why do we ignore it so much closer to home?

policy toward Cuba. The first wave of criticism broke in November 1972. In the aftermath of two particularly brutal hijackings on 29 October and 12 November, editorial writers of at least three major newspapers, the *New York Times*, the *Washington Post*, and the *Christian Science Monitor*, made nearly identical arguments for beginning talks with the Cubans.[2] All welcomed Premier Castro's offer to discuss a treaty dealing with the hijacking problem. None, however, felt that these talks should be an end in themselves. "Handled properly," the *Washington Post* argued, they could lead to "cultural exchanges, claims settlements, trade talks, and political relations. . . ." We must move on to other things, according to the *New York Times*; President Nixon, "the supreme pragmatist," surely knew that an OAS-U.S. policy of "diplomatic and economic quarantine" set up a decade ago "under totally different circumstances than those of today" was obsolete.

And what precisely were these altered circumstances? The *New York Times* mentioned one: Latin America was no longer interested in isolating Cuba. Peru and Chile had already resumed relations, and Mexico had never severed them. The four ex-British Caribbean states, Barbados, Jamaica, Guyana, and Trinidad-Tobago, had announced their desire to begin contacts with Cuba. And others were leaning in that direction. Why they should be doing this the *New York Times* did not say, but the *Christian Science Monitor* broadly hinted that the Latin American states were satisfied that Castro was no longer exporting revolution, especially after Che Guevara's failure in Bolivia in 1967. Another altered circumstance was Cuba's desirability as a base for Soviet strategic weapons. "So long as Mr. Nixon's deal with Russia holds," argued the *Monitor*, "the Russians are not going to put their strategic weapons into Cuba, or into any other place in the Americas." Finally, each newspaper made the point that has now become a revisionist rallying cry, namely, if we are seeking better relations with the major Communist states, why hold out on a nearby minor one? Why, the *Washington Post* asked in conclusion, should "the smallest and weakest of the Communist states alone be held at arm's length?"

These are still the major arguments advanced in the press for the resumption of relations, although there has been some embroidery on the familiar themes. The news columns, too, have contributed to the present atmosphere of support for negotiations. Many news items related to Cuba have been presented as portents favorable to renewed

---

[2] *New York Times*, 19 November 1972; *Washington Post*, 17 November 1972; *Christian Science Monitor*, 27 November 1972.

relations. The views of revisionist opinion leaders—for example, the twelve Republican representatives who called for "legislative and executive initiatives to consider the re-establishment of ties between Washington and Havana" in 1973[3]—have consistently been reported. Administration officials who support the "negotiate now" thesis have also been selectively quoted. For example, a Defense Intelligence Agency analyst testifying before the House Subcommittee on Inter-American Affairs was quoted to the effect that Cuba was no serious military threat to the United States.[4]

The second great wave of press speculation on America's Cuban policy came after Nixon's removal from office in August 1974.[5] The new administration, it was felt, would be more flexible since President Ford had no fixed prejudices about the Castro regime. In his 28 August 1974 press conference, the new chief executive did say that the United States would work with OAS members in dealing with Cuba —a statement hailed at the time as a "significant softening" of policy.[6] The hope placed in Mr. Ford's pragmatism was strengthened by fresh concern over this country's growing isolation from Latin America. This worry mounted visibly in the two weeks prior to the November 1974 meeting in Quito of the hemisphere's foreign ministers. That gathering was supposed to decide the question of the OAS sanctions imposed on Cuba in 1964. Most observers believed they would be lifted and that it was high time for the United States to adjust to the new reality.[7] When the effort to remove the sanctions failed (despite American neutrality), journalists argued that the vote was not even a Pyrrhic victory for the United States, but a setback for the OAS, an embarrassment to this country, and a useless pro-

---

[3] Charlotte Saikowski, *Christian Science Monitor*, 30 January 1973, and James Nelson Goodsell, *Christian Science Monitor*, 26 March 1973.

[4] Nicholas Daniloff, *Atlanta Journal and Constitution*, 4 February 1973. George Ball, in his 1964 speech, made precisely the same point—a fact overlooked in this piece.

[5] Press optimism about the former president's pragmatism in 1972 was soon replaced with exasperation over Nixon's inflexible insistence on keeping Cuba at arm's length. There were also numerous assertions about the influence of his "Cuban" friend Bebe Rebozo.

[6] Laurence Stern and Marilyn Berger, *Washington Post*, 29 August 1974. Also *Washington Star-News*, 29 August 1974, and Stan Carter, *New York Daily News*, 30 August 1974. Carter alone pointed out that Ford's formula differed in no way from Nixon's 1973 foreign policy report to the Congress: "in considering any change, we shall act in concert with our fellow members of the OAS."

[7] *Christian Science Monitor*, 5 November 1974; Joseph Novitski, *Washington Post*, 3 November 1974; *Baltimore Sun*, 9 November 1974. Even the conservative *Chicago Tribune*, 8 November 1974, felt it was "an idea whose time has come," but cautioned, "[w]e should sharply scrutinize the idea, its merits and its pitfalls."

longation of meaningless sanctions.[8] Finally, one more theme emerged after the Quito meeting. The *St. Louis Post-Dispatch*, among other papers, argued in an editorial that the United States was not only in danger of being isolated in Latin America, but of being isolated from precisely those regimes, the democratic ones, that should be our firmest friends.[9]

This critique of American policy has been supplemented by a stream of reports from American journalists visiting Cuba. Their impressions are favorable, in sharp contrast to the negative reactions of visitors in the 1960s who stressed shabbiness and economic distress. The revolution, we are now told, is a success: an overwhelming majority of Cubans support it, the economy has at long last recovered, education and public health programs are proof of the regime's concern for the poor. Model projects like the Instituto Lenin, a high school, and Alamar, a housing scheme for peasant families, even Havana's ice cream parlor, are lovingly evoked again and again. And incipient Cuban democracy is hinted at in descriptions of "the secret, popular elections" held in Matanzas province in November 1974. Meanwhile, harsher issues like prisoners, rationing, and dependence on the Soviet Union are downplayed or omitted entirely. In short, the point is that the Cuban regime is permanent and progressive and American opposition is outdated and perhaps counterproductive.[10]

Cuba Seen by the Academy. The American press, of course, is not alone responsible for the current climate of opinion. The academy too has contributed arguments, some in anticipation, some in echo, of the editorial page. Certainly the earliest and most thoughtful of the intellectuals is John Plank. In an article written for the *New York Times* (March 1969), Professor Plank argued that American policy toward Cuba was not a failure. It had served its purpose over the years, but it had also helped Castro to stay in power since he could blame his economic failure on the American embargo. In the meantime, Plank argued, the Cuban leader has made a success of the revolution by retaining his popularity and getting most Cubans to accept the legitimacy of a socialist revolution. In Latin America there

---

[8] *Baltimore Sun*, 13 November 1974. The *Chicago Tribune* agreed that a weakened OAS was a Castro victory (15 November 1974).

[9] *St. Louis Post-Dispatch*, 13 November 1974.

[10] See, for example, Terri Shaw, *Washington Post*, 29 December 1974; 30 December 1974; 31 December 1974; 2 January 1975; Ted Morgan, "Cuba," *New York Times Sunday Magazine*, 1 December 1974, p. 27; David Binder, *New York Times*, 4 October 1974 and 22 October 1974; John E. Cooney, *Wall Street Journal*, 4 December 1974 and 16 December 1974.

has been a reassessment of the isolation policy, not out of increased interest in communism, but out of doubt about the efficacy of isolation.

Two particular aspects of present policy seem worthy of revision according to Plank. First, our presence at Guantánamo. Plank denies its military usefulness: "it frightens no one, the base is militarily insignificant in today's world, . . . our presence there is justified on grounds more of sentiment than of security."[11] To Castro it is not a believable threat, but it is an excellent whipping boy for *fidelista* propaganda. The second policy worth reexamining is restriction of trade and travel. Plank argues that while the embargo was not designed to overthrow the regime, it was expected to do Castro serious damage. In truth, it has not done that as long as the Soviet Union has paid the bills, and he implies that the burden on the Kremlin has been exaggerated. The Russian contribution is certainly not much more, he argues, than the United States transfers to Puerto Rico in direct federal payments. Moreover, the Russians are being helped out by increasing Western European and Japanese trade with Cuba.

If present policy is wanting, what then are our choices? Plank first considers the even tougher measures advocated by the American Security Council and the Citizens Committee for a Free Cuba. Their first choice is a tighter economic blockade around the island. But that would be an act of war which would bring us into confrontation with Cuba and its powerful ally. Moreover, it would cause dissension at home and increase friction with our own allies. The second choice is "a clean, surgical operation," that is, an invasion, which Plank objects to on moral grounds and possibly military ones. Such intervention would probably be costly since Castro has succeeded in forging a nation, a people who would resist. That leaves accommodation. This process, however, would not be easy and could only advance by "incremental steps." It might begin with a dialogue on hijacking, followed by an adjustment of U.S. and Cuban property claims. Plank does not refer here to the large corporate claims which have already been written off as losses, but to the smaller unsatisfied claims of U.S. citizens in amounts varying from $20,000 to $50,000. On the Cuban side, there are a reasonable number of blocked assets to adjudicate. The third incremental step would be a relaxation of

---

[11] John Plank, "We Should Start Talking with Castro," *New York Times Sunday Magazine*, 30 March 1969, and reprinted in Richard B. Gray, ed., *Latin America and the United States in the 1970s* (Ithasca, Ill.: F. E. Peacock Co., 1971), pp. 241-52.

travel and trade restrictions, and finally a reincorporation of Cuba into the American family of nations.

John Plank then turns to a cost-benefit analysis of resuming relations. The costs, he warns, would be heavy—not in strategic terms, but in both political and ideological terms. We would have to accept the bitter facts that Castro's regime is a success and that our new policy would anger conservative Latin American regimes. Moreover, a good part of American public opinion wouldn't accept it. Plank predicts a hysterical reaction from the Cuban community in the United States. The benefits, however, clearly outweigh the costs. First, renewed relations would remove a point of tension between the two superpowers. Second, they would open the way for Cuba's rejoining the OAS. In addition, Cuba would be brought into the emerging Caribbean community—a necessary development if that community is to prosper. Two additional benefits would be the end of hijackings and the reduced isolation of the Cuban people. But Plank warns that accommodation will not simply happen. It must be worked at—indeed, initiated by—the United States. The academic community as a whole has shared this view, and a number of specialists have been even more critical than Plank of American policy.[12]

Congress and Cuba. Quite recently the call for revision has also been heard in Congress and even in the executive branch. Some, like Senator Fulbright and Senator Kennedy, have long advocated a new policy. Others, Senator Robert C. Byrd, for instance, while expressing reservations, have called for review if not revision of our Cuban policy guided by "enlightened self-interest."[13] In the last year, too, a staff member of the Senate Foreign Relations Committee visited Cuba and submitted a report recommending an end to the trade embargo and relaxation of travel restrictions, particularly for Cuban diplomats at the United Nations.[14]

---

[12] See the transcript of the Congressional Conference on U.S.-Cuba Relations, 19-20 April 1972, especially the comments of Brady Tyson (American University), pp. 85-88, and Lawrence Birns (New School for Social Research), pp. 98-100.
[13] See the remarks of Senator Byrd reprinted in the *Congressional Record*, 12 March 1973, pp. S4334-35.
[14] Pat Holt, *Cuba: A Staff Report*, U.S. Congress, Senate, Committee on Foreign Relations, 93rd Congress, 2nd session, 2 August 1974. This eleven-page report is so inept that it inspires only one question: was this trip necessary? As an example of the report's naivete, it assures its readers on page 2 that in 1973 per capita income in Cuba was $1,587, "by far the highest in Latin America with the possible exception of Venezuela where everything is distorted by oil." This is nonsense on a spectacular scale—an observation confirmed by the per capita figure of 561 pesos (also for 1973) revealed by Raul Castro a few months earlier

The congressional initiative that garnered the most publicity was the Javits-Pell mission to Havana in October 1974. The two senators, both members of the Foreign Relations Committee, spent four days in Cuba speaking to officials including Castro. The trip was undertaken "pursuant to the Javits-Pell amendment to the State Department authorization bill (Section 14), calling for a review of United States' Cuba policy by the Congress and the President." That amendment was passed by the Senate on 23 April 1974.[15] Senators Javits and Pell recommended small measures (dropping travel restrictions, for example) to tempt the Cubans into reciprocation. Their report suggested that, once some reciprocal gesture had been obtained, the trade embargo should be relaxed on a product-by-product basis to build up negotiating momentum.

Probably the most significant phenomenon, however, is the remarkable turnabout in U.S. public opinion. In the last two years, according to the Harris poll, a majority of Americans have begun to favor resuming relations with Cuba.[16] The four arguments for resuming relations most often cited by respondents were: (1) differences should be resolved through negotiation; to further ignore Cuba would only widen the gap between us; (2) the Castro regime is apparently in power to stay; (3) détente with the Soviet Union and China makes our Cuban policy inconsistent; and (4) renewed relations might help reduce the price of sugar.[17]

Congress, the press, and the American people obviously have a great deal to say about whether or not we resume relations with

---

in an interview with a Yugoslav journal, *Kommunist*. Even making the extremely generous assumption that the peso equals the dollar and that Raul Castro was telling the truth, the staff report missed Cuba's real per capita income by nearly a factor of three. See *Bohemia* (Havana), 15 March 1974, pp. 50-54.

[15] Jacob Javits and Claiborne Pell, "The United States and Cuba: A Propitious Moment," U.S. Congress, Senate, Committee on Foreign Relations, 93rd Congress, 2nd session, October 1974. See also Senator Pell's article in the *Miami Herald*, 20 October 1974.

[16] *Chicago Tribune*, 16 December 1974. The figures for 1973 were 51 percent favoring relations, 33 percent opposed. In 1974 they were 50 percent and 34 percent. The question was phrased as follows: "It is argued that since the war in Vietnam is over and relations with Communist Russia and China are getting better, the United States ought to reestablish diplomatic relations with Cuba. Others say as long as Cuba is ruled by Fidel Castro, we should not have anything to do with her. Do you favor or oppose establishing diplomatic relations with Cuba?"

[17] Secretary of Agriculture Earl Butz apparently agrees with this argument. In an interview on ABC television, he favored dropping the trade embargo in order to buy Cuban sugar and thus reduce the price. He also felt Cuba would make a good market for American rice. *New York Times*, 25 November 1974.

Cuba. But the actual negotiations must still be carried out by U.S. government officials and their Cuban counterparts. And that brings us to the question: how do the principals now see each other?

Signals, Noise and Preconditions for Negotiations

Before going on to discuss our Cuba policy in the 1970s, we must pause to examine the concept of "signals" in international relations. The critics of our position are highly frustrated by what seems to them U.S. officialdom's appalling ignorance of the fact that something is wrong—even Belshazzar had the sense to call in his academics to read the writing on the wall.[18] One demonstration of the government's insensitivity, these critics believe, is that various signals emitted by the Cuban regime have not received adequate response from the United States.

After his return from Havana, for example, Senator McGovern urged the State Department to answer a clear signal sent by Castro. "The next move is clearly up to us, and the ball is back in our court. This is a very significant change in the position of the government."[19] McGovern's statement raises a number of interlocking questions. What precisely was the change in Cuban policy to which McGovern referred? Was it significant? For that matter, just what is a signal? Surely it is in the nature of "signals"—indeed, of all esoteric types of communication—to be ambiguous. To claim that they are clear, simple, and not susceptible to varying interpretation is to pretend to an expertise that no man, not even a United States senator, possesses. The recent McGovern visit and its immediate aftermath are an excellent demonstration of this point.

It is clear that Fidel Castro was intent on treating the senator from South Dakota with utmost cordiality, in contrast to the two earlier visitors from the U.S. Senate. Nevertheless, "the significant change" reported by McGovern seems less significant at second glance. According to official Cuban summaries of the press conference at which the alleged change was announced, the Cuban premier stated that lifting the embargo is still a precondition for negotiations because Cuba cannot "negotiate under pressure." In replying to a journalist's question, Castro did admit that there had been "some small gestures" on the part of the United States, but he also said that Cuba had already made "much more important and much more

---

[18] Dan. 5:7 and 13:17.
[19] Quoted in *Washington Post*, 14 May 1975.

valuable" gestures, such as solving the hijacking problem—a gesture, he argued, which has not received a proper American reply. Such a reply, he suggested, might consist of removing U.S. restrictions on the export of food and medicine. But when asked directly if a limited lifting of the embargo would lead to negotiations, Castro made the following critical point: Cuba preferred the elimination of the entire embargo, but a "sufficiently broad" elimination might help improve relations. He reiterated this point by stating that a partial end to the embargo would be "an important step" towards Cuba's review of its relations with this country. But he did not indicate that such a move would necessarily be enough to initiate talks. As we shall see later, this was not, in fact, a departure from Castro's earlier statements. Nevertheless, Castro did make an impressive appeal to the American audience by speaking at one point in English: "We wish friendship. We belong to two different worlds but we are neighbors. One way or another we owe it to ourselves to live in peace." [20]

With that, Senator McGovern returned to the United States. Were Castro's statements at the press conference a clear signal? On the following day, the Cuban leader delivered a major address in Havana celebrating the thirtieth anniversary of the ending of World War II. This speech, ignored by the American press, was essentially a hymn of praise to the Soviet Union for its victory over Nazi Germany. In Castro's words: "the true, historic and unquestionable fact is that it was precisely the Soviet people and the Soviet Army who carried the main and decisive weight in the defeat of fascism." [21] The U.S. contribution to the allied victory was not mentioned, though Castro did say that U.S. cities had escaped untouched and American capitalists had made $100 billion in profits. The American role after the war, however, did not go without mention. In the strident tones he used to employ routinely in the early 1960s, Castro blamed the cold war entirely on the "imperialists" who were resisted only by the Soviet Union. The latter had also made possible the freeing of

---

[20] Quoted in *New York Times*, 9 May 1975. The importance of the most recent American signal—a State Department announcement permitting, among other things, trade with Cuba by foreign subsidiaries of U.S. corporations—has also been exaggerated. For the most part, this new measure merely accepts what has already happened—an action which neatly parallels the earlier U.S. acceptance of the San José foreign ministers' decision. See *Wall Street Journal*, 22 August 1975, and *New York Times*, 22 August 1975. Meanwhile, the Cuban leader called the announcement a "positive action," but pressed for the lifting of the direct trade embargo. *Washington Post*, 23 August 1975.

[21] Radio Havana, 9 May 1975, as reported in *FBIS Daily Report, Latin America*, 10 May 1975.

subject colonial peoples and the "definitive victory of the heroic cause of the Vietnamese people." He added:

> If today the imperialists, with their energy and raw material crises, with knives in their mouths, are not trying to distribute among themselves the natural resources of the world, if they are not trying to punish any nationalizations, if they are not trying to grab those resources, it is simply because there exists the Soviet Union and the socialist camp.[22]

The juxtaposition of these views, expressed by the Cuban leader on consecutive days, raises some rather profound questions about the nature of signals. What, after all, is a signal and what is noise? Or do both serve purposes in Cuban negotiating strategy that decision makers in this country dare not ignore?

The Shift in American Policy

In examining the Cuban policy elaborated by the Nixon administration we must distinguish carefully between the president's personal views and the formal documents carrying his name. There is still much confusion over the extent to which American policy under Nixon was based on rational considerations and the extent to which it derived from personal spleen. The contrast between the formal and the informal Nixon is particularly instructive in this case since the former president was usually described as Castro's archenemy.

The 1971 foreign policy report to Congress was plain and unsparing: Cuba continues to rule itself out of the inter-American system by its subversion in Latin America, by its military ties with the Soviet Union, and by its "unremitting hostility" toward this country.[23] A year later, the president advised the Congress that although there had been "moderation of its rhetoric and more selectivity in its approach to exporting revolution . . . these seem to be only a shift in tactics prompted by the consistent failures of its domestic policy and revolutionary adventures."[24] Money, arms, and training were still being supplied to subversive groups in Latin America. Moreover, according to the report, Cuba's military ties with

---

22 Ibid.

23 *U.S. Foreign Policy for the 1970s: Building for Peace.* A Report to the Congress by Richard M. Nixon (Washington, D.C.: U.S. Government Printing Office, 25 February 1971), and reprinted in the *Department of State Bulletin*, 22 March 1971.

24 *U.S. Foreign Policy for the 1970s: Emerging Structure of Peace* (Washington, D.C.: U.S. Government Printing Office, 9 February 1972), pp. 96-97.

the Soviet Union were increasing, with more arms imports and the "provision of facilities" otherwise unspecified.[25] The 1973 report, nearly a duplicate of the previous year's, reminded the Congress that the United States could not act unilaterally in this matter. "We will consider a change in policy toward Cuba when Cuba changes its policy toward the other countries of the hemisphere," the president concluded, "but in considering any change, we shall act in concert with our fellow members of the OAS." [26]

Nixon's less formal statements are more revealing. On the one hand, they seem firmer, and on the other, more specific as to what the United States finds unacceptable about the Cuban regime. The firmness came out clearly in a conversation with Dan Rather televised on 2 January 1972. After stating his belief that Castro had not receded "one inch from his determination" to export revolution, Nixon added under further questioning from Rather that he did not expect "dialogue" with Cuba to be possible. The president explained:

> We follow Mr. Castro's activities, his public speeches and the like, very, very closely; and he thrives, since he has made virtually a basket case of Cuba economically, in stirring up trouble in other countries. He couldn't possibly survive, in my opinion, unless he had this policy of "foreign devils." [27]

Nixon's assertion that Castro's xenophobia was purely utilitarian raises a fascinating (and apparently unconsidered) possibility that would have been perfectly consistent with the president's logic: namely, a rapid, unilateral attempt at rapprochement with Fidel Castro designed to deprive him of his necessary devil. That opportunity was neglected, but in the interview Nixon also made clear that his difficulty with Cuba was not objection to the nature of the regime: if the Cubans wished to be Communists, then so be it. Finally, the chief executive was aware of the charge that non-relations with Cuba made no sense in an era of détente. Relations with any country depend on its attitudes toward us, he said. "Cuba is engaged in a constant program of belligerence toward the United States" while the Chinese Communists "are now ready to talk about their role in Asia and our role in Asia." [28]

---

[25] Ibid., p. 97.

[26] U.S. Foreign Policy for the 1970s: Shaping a Durable Peace (Washington, D.C.: U.S. Government Printing Office, 3 May 1973), p. 121.

[27] Reprinted in Department of State Bulletin, 25 January 1972, p. 84. This view was repeated in an interview with Garnett Horner, White House correspondent for the Washington Star, and reprinted in New York Times, 10 November 1972.

[28] Department of State Bulletin, 24 January 1972, p. 84.

The State Department under Nixon. Recent Cuban policy, of course, was not the exclusive province of Richard Nixon. The most articulate official since George Ball on this problem has been Robert A. Hurwitch, deputy assistant secretary for inter-American affairs in the early 1970s and now ambassador to the Dominican Republic. In testimony to the Senate Foreign Relations Committee in September 1971 and March 1973, he most ably defended recent American policy. First, Hurwitch reminded his audience that the objective of the United States is not subversion of Cuba, but "the reduction of Cuba's capability to export armed revolution and the discouragement of Soviet adventures in this hemisphere." He was equally at pains to assure the committee that our policy was under "constant review" and that respect for "diversity abroad" was an extension of our native pluralism. Nevertheless, Cuba remained our special *bête noire* because of subversion, military ties to the Russians, and hostility toward the United States. On subversion, Hurwitch admitted that Castro was more "cautious," "selective," and "sophisticated" than he used to be, but that this was a result of failure rather than of a fundamental questioning of the goal itself. On the matter of military links with the Kremlin, Hurwitch argued that they were tighter than ever. This time, however, he attempted to spell out what was meant by "military ties"—a phrase that had long escaped definition:

> We obviously do not question Cuba's right to maintain an army, or equip it or to receive training. Every nation has such a right. What concerns us is Cuba's disposition to cooperate in the strategic goals of an extra-hemispheric "super-power." This was illustrated by the emplacement of offensive missiles in October, 1962, and more recently by Cuba's cooperation in 1970 in Soviet efforts to establish a nuclear submarine facility at Cienfuegos, which, had it succeeded, could have caused a major disturbance in the hemisphere. Any disturbance, even a slight one, of the balance of military power with the Soviet Union, must remain of concern to us even as our efforts to develop peaceful contacts with that country continue.[29]

Hurwitch's testimony in 1973 dealt with four arguments favoring resumed relations. First, he refuted the need for symmetry in détente by showing with what little eagerness the Cubans have pursued the idea of rapprochement. Moreover, there was the brute fact that at least some kind of relationship was necessary with the Communist giants, while unavoidable business could be conducted with

---

[29] Reprinted in the *Department of State Bulletin*, 11 October 1971, p. 392.

Cuba on an ad hoc basis; he cited the hijacking accord and the 1965 refugee airlift agreement as instances of just that. Second, despite declining Latin support for the OAS economic sanctions, Hurwitch contended that there were still not enough votes to repeal them—a belief borne out at the Quito meeting. Third, he doubted that the United States had much to gain in trade since "Cuba is heavily mortgaged economically to the Soviet Union for many years to come and there is no foreseeable way it can produce the foreign exchange to again become an important purchaser in the United States market"—despite the current high level of prices for sugar and nickel.[30] Finally, Hurwitch responded to the argument that Soviet links to Cuba could be severed only after Cuban suspicion of the United States had been allayed by conciliatory gestures from us: this belief, he said, did not square with reality. Quite apart from security concerns, in recent years the Cubans have locked themselves "into a dependent relationship with the Soviet Union in every sense— economic, political, military, and cultural."[31]

Moreover, conciliatory gestures from the United States, according to Hurwitch, would "convince Fidel Castro that his course has been correct all along," and *fidelistas* would be encouraged to subvert vulnerable Latin American regimes.[32] Senate Resolution 160, which would call upon the president to initiate rapprochement, Hurwitch said, would enhance Castro's prestige and leave the impression that the United States no longer takes its neighbors' subversive activities very seriously.[33] Despite the growing expectation outside official circles that major changes were imminent, in public U.S. policy makers remained skeptical of Cuba's willingness to change and disinclined to grant what would amount to concessions to the Castro government.

U.S. Policy in the Last Year. In this last year, however, American officials have sent out a new set of very complex signals that are at least the beginnings of a shift in policy. Unfortunately, more tends to be read into these signals than should be. The result has been the impression, widespread in the last fifteen months, that serious talks were about to begin. This misinterpretation is rooted in two simple assumptions: that American policy makers are saying and doing less

---

[30] U.S. Congress, Senate, Statement by Robert A. Hurwitch to the Subcommittee on Inter-American Affairs, Committee on Foreign Relations, 26 March 1973, p. 3 (mimeo).

[31] Ibid., pp. 4-6.

[32] Ibid., p. 4 and p. 6.

[33] Ibid., p. 4 and p. 7.

in public than they are saying and doing in private and that their signals are directed at a single audience. In fact, American officials have been communicating with six audiences. The first, the U.S. Congress, included thirty-four senators definitely opposed to a quick resumption of relations and a smaller group in favor. The other interested parties were the Cuban exile community, the Latin American countries that wanted Cuba back in the community (Venezuela and Mexico, in particular), Latin nations (chiefly Chile and Uruguay) that remained hostile to Castro, the Soviet Union, and finally Cuba itself.[34]

Cuba is no mere bilateral problem, and American policy has begun to shift *because* the issue has become multilateral in scope. In the last year, there are indications that part of our Cuban policy has become subordinated to the overall Latin American strategy. That broad policy, the New Dialogue, is grounded in our need to take Latin America more seriously than we have in the recent past. In order to keep the dialogue going, the United States seems to be willing to make concessions when Latin interests are affected. After a certain amount of controversy had developed in Argentina, the U.S. Treasury permitted American subsidiaries there to export motor vehicles to Cuba. On a broader front, the United States maintained quiet neutrality at the Quito meeting and raised no objections to Cuba's participation in the cancelled Buenos Aires meeting of foreign ministers.

Furthermore, all has not been quiet on the bilateral front. Officials have recently softened their publicly expressed views on Cuba. They seldom condemn Cuban behavior outright, as they used to, and no longer stress the regime's continued belligerence toward this country. Moreover, there are occasional hints that talks will be possible when the Cubans are in the mood, and expectations of "movement" on the Cuban problem in the near future have been expressed.[35]

In his most recent major address on Latin America (1 March 1975), Secretary of State Henry Kissinger summed up official American feeling on Cuba. After reassuring his Houston audience that the United States will not move until the OAS sanctions are lifted, he read the key paragraph:

> We see no virtue in perpetual antagonism between the United States and Cuba. Our concerns relate above all to

---

34 *New York Times*, 6 May 1974.

35 See Secretary Kissinger's statement to a Senate Subcommittee on Appropriations in *Diario de las Americas* (Miami), 26 July 1974; *Diario de las Americas*, 21 August 1974.

Cuba's external policies and military relationships with countries outside the Hemisphere. We have taken some symbolic steps to indicate that we are prepared to move in a new direction if Cuba will. Fundamental change cannot come, however, unless Cuba demonstrates a readiness to assume the mutuality of obligation and regard upon which a new relationship must be founded.[36]

Privately, American officials have minimized the material gain to be won from renewed relations. As one State Department spokesman put it, the only advantage would be "having put the past behind us." In the meantime, what they would like to see develop would seem to be, first, conciliatory gestures from the Cubans such as the release of important political prisoners, second, third-country mediation, and third, Cuban good behavior at the next foreign ministers' meeting.

The Shift in Cuba's Policy

Havana's interest in talks is also recent.[37] But unlike the United States, Cuba has made both its signals and its conditions clear. One of the first signals came in late September 1972. In the course of a press interview, Fidel Castro played on the already familiar theme of not talking to the United States while Nixon remained in office.[38]

---

[36] *Department of State Press Release*, no. 108 (1 March 1975), p. 6.

[37] As recently as April 1971, Fidel Castro delivered an anti-American blast worthy of his earlier and more youthful efforts. But even Castro's tirades are instructive. After listing American crimes against Cuba since 1898, Castro summed up his feelings: "What kind of normal relations or arrangements can there be between a revolutionary country such as Cuba . . . and this Yankee imperialism, this genocidal government, this cop-like government, this aggressive government. Reconciliation and normal relations with Mr. Nixon would mean that Cuba was renouncing its solidarity with the revolutionary movements and peoples and governments. But Cuba will not renounce this—we repeat this once more—will never renounce this solidarity." Then he asked his audience rhetorically: "Normal relations with the imperialists who are threatening our brother nations, who are a threat to other revolutions? How can this be if we are sworn to go and fight alongside our brothers against those same imperialists and against their mercenaries? How can anyone conceive of the idea of reconciliation or of normal relations with these same imperialists? Never, not at all." As for the American conditions for negotiations, Castro declared with some insight: "Of course, the old insolent and disrespectful language is no longer used by those who at one time thought they would have us on our knees. Now they almost seem to pine for a gesture from Cuba. But such a gesture, Mr. Nixon— and we say this with all the honesty which characterizes this revolution and its statements—will never be made." Radio Havana, 19 April 1971, reported in *FBIS Daily Report, Latin America*, 20 April 1971.

[38] The Cuban premier characterized President Nixon as "shameless, a demagogue and a faker." Pedro Martínez Pirez, "Fidel Castro on Possible Talks with U.S.," 30 September 1972, Prensa Latina (mimeo).

Moreover, according to Castro, in any discussion with Washington, Cuba would not place self-interest above the interests of Latin America. He added: "Because of our own interests, we're not going to forget about the imperialist role of gendarme in Latin America. . . . I think that when the day comes that the U.S. becomes realistic and ceases to be a gendarme in Latin America, relations between them and us may improve." [39] Having settled that point, Castro set down three conditions for negotiations: first, "the economic blockade must be brought to an end, with no strings attached"; second, the United States "must get out of the Guantánamo base"; third, it must stop "all subversive activities." And, he added, all of this must be done unconditionally. "That does not mean that we would commit ourselves to anything in exchange for that, nor that when we hold discussions we would discuss only Cuba." [40]

For the next fifteen months these terms remained unchanged or were stated more harshly.[41] At times they were simply forgotten as Castro preached the gospel of no compromise with the forces of darkness. But a curious incident in January 1974 led to a new version of his conditions for negotiations. In a press interview, the Cuban

---

[39] Ibid., p. 11.

[40] Ibid.

[41] The following month Castro repeated these conditions before a larger audience and in harsher language: "We are not interested in relations with a gendarme state. We are a part of Latin America, and someday we will be part of the Latin America community. The minimum requirement for an improvement in Cuba's relations with the United States is that Yankee imperialism cease to be a gendarme in this hemisphere . . . a power that imposes counterrevolution and repression in this continent against the progressive and popular movements. . . .

"And then there's the criminal war in Vietnam. We fail to see how our relations with the United States can possibly improve, considering our solidarity with Vietnam, our constant relentless condemnation of the crimes being perpetrated there. . . . But even when the war in Vietnam has come to an end, there still remains the situation in Latin America. We don't demand, we don't establish as a prerequisite, that there be a socialist or even a progressive government in the United States, but at least there should be a *realistic* government, a government that will recognize the present world balance of power, a government that will realize that it is in no shape to continue playing the role of world gendarme. . . .

"As long as the government of the U.S.—no matter who is in the White House—carries on a policy of counterrevolution in Latin America, a policy of repression, crimes, torture, harassment, blockade, and repression of the popular and other revolutionary movements, our relations with the U.S. cannot improve— not the people, with whom our relations are steadily improving." Speech delivered upon receiving the Frederic Joliot-Curie Medal from the World Peace Council and reprinted in *Granma Weekly Review* (Havana), 22 October 1972, p. 12. In his 26 July 1973 speech, Castro made no mention of conditions or the possibility of negotiating with this country. Radio Havana, 26 July 1973, reported in *FBIS Daily Report, Latin America,* 27 July 1973.

ambassador to Mexico stated that his country was not waging "a holy war" against the United States, that Cuba rarely breaks relations with anyone, and that Cuba had never refused to negotiate with the Americans. The only condition he laid down was the ending of the American trade embargo.[42] The ambassador's statement, of course, caused a press sensation in Mexico which led the Cuban foreign ministry to issue a "clarifying note." Though the note was much harsher in tone, it did repeat the basic signal that had come out of Mexico.[43]

One month later, in an interview with the Mexican left-wing magazine *Siempre*, Fidel Castro provided his own clarification. Yes, the foreign ministry's note had been necessary to counter "distortions" following the ambassador's statements. In fact, Cuba was really in no hurry to begin negotiations. "We can wait ten or twenty years. I say that, in so far as relations with the United States are concerned, we can wait." Then he offered a new view of the "blockade," a theme that would be developed in subsequent months: the American embargo had hurt Cuba, but it was increasingly discredited; the United States was becoming isolated on this issue, and it was in America's interest to drop it. Nevertheless, despite this flock of caveats, Castro did not formally repudiate the new formula for conditions.[44] Six months later, in an interview with Panamanian journalists, Castro reiterated the single condition signal:

> [We] have declared that we are prepared to talk with the United States when the economic blockade ceases. We have established as a prior condition that the blockade cease because there can be no conditions between the one who blockades and the one who is blockaded. As a prior condition for any negotiation between the United States and us, the economic blockade must unquestionably cease. That is our position.[45]

---

[42] *FBIS Daily Report, Latin America*, 9 January 1974.

[43] The ministry's note nevertheless placed the entire blame for bad relations on the United States and demanded an unconditional lifting of the "blockade." It added that Guantánamo will be the "main point of any bilateral dialogue between the two nations," although the base "lacks strategic importance as far as Cuban national defense is concerned." *FBIS Daily Report, Latin America*, 11 January 1974.

[44] Luis Suárez, *Siempre* (Mexico City), 20 February 1974, pp. 18-23. Later in the interview, in commenting on exile groups and terrorist activities Castro passed up an opportunity to blame the CIA. "The CIA no longer controls some of those buzzards. No, I don't think the CIA is doing those things; but they are being done by the 'little cadres' trained by the CIA." This is, I believe, the first opportunity the Cuban premier has missed.

[45] *FBIS Daily Report, Latin America*, 27 August 1974.

In recent months the formula on conditions has remained fundamentally the same, although there have been interesting variations. In a televised interview for CBS, Castro strongly reiterated the single precondition, an assertion he repeated for *L'Humanité*, the French Communist daily.[46] The variations include a somewhat benign view of Gerald Ford. "We see Ford with a certain hope in the sense that he may after all adopt a different policy toward Cuba," he explained to CBS.[47] In January 1975, Castro also informed Mexican newsmen that although President Ford held views similar to Nixon's, he had "no personal links with the counter-revolution." Castro added: "Nixon had an almost personal hatred against the Cuban revolution, but I have no reason to believe that Ford does." [48]

The second variation is the number of admiring remarks made by Castro about Secretary Kissinger. In his warmest accolade to date, the Cuban leader remarked to *Oui* magazine: "In general, we think highly of Kissinger. He is intelligent and realistic and truly able. So we are favorably disposed toward him." [49] Among other things, this is the highest tribute a Cuban official has yet paid any American official. And despite Castro's verbosity, he is usually careful in his choice of words, especially in interviews. Thus the adjectives "realistic and intelligent" are not arbitrary compliments. In the Castro Marxist lexicon, a Western leader who is realistic understands the nature of the present epoch: namely, that the forces of peace, progress, and socialism are winning the struggle against capitalism. American imperialism is doomed; and the realistic leader accepts the inevitable and thus avoids war in an attempt to make the best terms possible. Castro considers Kissinger, whom he has compared to Metternich, the perfect embodiment of the realistic statement.[50]

In summary then, the Cuban leader's interest in negotiations is now over a year old, dating back to early January 1974 when the

46 *New York Times*, 22 October 1974, and *L'Humanité* (Paris), 24 October 1974, p. 2.

47 *New York Times*, 22 October 1974.

48 *FBIS Daily Report, Latin America*, 6 January 1975; *Newsweek*, 9 September 1974, pp. 40-41.

49 The interview was reprinted in ARA-PAF Press Clips (Department of State), 13 December 1974.

50 The reference to Metternich was first made in remarks to a group of Argentine businessmen and reported in *O Globo* (Rio de Janeiro), 2 March 1974, p. 11. Castro on that occasion said: "Like Metternich, Kissinger is a minister of foreign relations of an empire whose policy is based on the survival of the empire because he knows that it is in crisis. Kissinger is an intelligent man who tries to adapt the foreign policy of the United States to the reality of today with the primary objective of preserving the Yankee empire as long as possible."

regime first laid down comparatively moderate conditions for negotiations. That raises an interesting question. Why did the change take place just then? Does the answer tell us something about the nature of the switch itself?

January 1974 happens to have been the date of the arrival of the general secretary of the Soviet Communist party in Havana after a long and unexplained delay. Had the Soviet leaders placed pressure on the Cubans to be more friendly to the United States? Did they exact, as the price for a high-level Soviet visit, a demonstrable softening of Havana's position? The timing seems too perfect to have been coincidence. If it wasn't coincidence, American policy makers must assume that Cuba's recent willingness to talk is, at least in part, a result of direct Soviet pressure.[51]

One final point on the business of signalling. It is clear that the Cubans are looking for direct, high-level talks. The American industrialist Cyrus Eaton, who spoke with Castro twice in early 1974, confirmed this.[52] Intermediaries—whether congressmen, journalists, or businessmen—will not be particularly welcome to the Cubans in regard to furthering the prospect of negotiations. That does not mean that their visits may not be useful from an American standpoint; while it is true that little can be learned from these trips, they may help put negotiations more on our terms. However, it should not be surprising if reports coming out of Havana indicate Cuban irritation at unofficial intermediaries.

---

[51] For Soviet strategy on this issue, see below.
[52] See Eaton's reports in *Washington Post*, 12 February 1974, and *New York Times*, 13 February 1974.

5

NEGOTIATIONS: THE INTERESTS, OBJECTIVES, AND STRATEGIES OF THE PRINCIPALS

The Soviet Stake in the Negotiations

Even without direct Latin American involvement, our talks with Cuba can never be purely bilateral. "The problem of U.S.-Cuban relations," as William Ratliff quite correctly put it, "is in reality a problem of U.S.-Cuban-Soviet relations."[1] Therefore, it is proper to examine here the Soviet stake in the coming negotiations. There is something unnatural about the Soviet-Cuban alliance,[2] and while America's long-range interest lies in the rupture of this relationship, we must understand its nature before we are about the business of destroying it.

In general, the Soviet leaders have much to be grateful for in 1975 regarding Cuba. A decade ago the Soviet Union, after a long, cautious courtship, found itself in a very expensive marriage with an erratic, tempestuous partner who was not above embarrassing its mate in front of friends and enemies alike. Today that marriage, while not completely free of occasional spats, is a success and operates on the terms originally desired by the senior partner. Before 1968 the Kremlin could never be sure of Cuban support in the international arena. In Latin America, Castro was a notorious opponent of the old-line, pro-Soviet Communist parties—which had never been the last word in revolutionary chic. And at the 1966 Tricontinental Conference he seriously embarrassed Moscow by packing the con-

---

[1] William E. Ratliff, "Cuba and Hijacking and You," *New York Times*, 30 December 1972.

[2] Even the Russians have remarked on this, albeit indirectly. Brezhnev, in his Havana speech, pointed out: "Cuba is separated by thousands of kilometers from its friends in the socialist countries of Europe and Asia. But such is the nature of socialist internationalism that revolutionary Cuba has never been and never will be alone." Quoted in *Pravda*, 31 December 1974, p. 4.

gress (without Soviet prior knowledge, much less approval) with guerrilla representatives who shared his distaste for Russia's Communist allies in Latin America.[3] Since 1968 Castro has become a far more orthodox supporter of Soviet foreign policy.[4] He endorsed (with some qualifications) the Russian invasion of Czechoslovakia, defended the Russians vociferously at the Algerian congress of the nonaligned nations in 1973, and has warmly praised the Bolshevik Revolution on every suitable occasion.[5] Moreover, the Castro regime has begun to rely on the centralized planning apparatus favored by the Soviet Union, rather than the erratic decision-making style of its commander in chief.[6]

The principal Soviet objective now is to preserve the newly orthodox "island of freedom." If nothing else, a new member of the socialist camp must be a boost in morale for the post-Stalinist Soviet leadership. The Soviet Union's commitment to preserving the Cuban regime does not rest exclusively on ideological grounds, however. The Soviet Union has a long-term economic agreement with Cuba that, as it now stands, runs until 2011, by which time Cuba's multibillion-dollar debt will have been repaid. There is little doubt that the Russians intend to collect.[7]

How to preserve the regime does present a problem. Unlike Czechoslovakia, Cuba cannot be marched into with the help of friends in the Warsaw Pact. Instead, the Soviet leaders must rely on three

---

[3] See D. Bruce Jackson, *Castro, the Kremlin and Communism in Latin America* (Baltimore: Johns Hopkins Press, 1969), pp. 68-94.

[4] The complete story of Castro's "conversion" to Muscovite orthodoxy is still something of a mystery. Most observers believe that by 1967, after the Tricontinental episode, the Soviet leaders demanded more for their money and backed up their demand with a slowing down of vital oil supplies followed by hard bargaining on a new trade protocol between October 1967 and March 1968. Edward Gonzales, "Relationship with the Soviet Union," in Carmelo Mesa-Lago, ed., *Revolutionary Change in Cuba* (Pittsburgh: University of Pittsburgh Press, 1971), pp. 93-97.

[5] See, for example, the editorial in *Granma Weekly Review* (Havana), 17 November 1974, p. 1, "Long Live the Great October Socialist Revolution." It said in part: "The Great October Socialist Revolution made it possible for 100 million men to become for the first time builders of their future and raise the triumphant banner of socialism over one-sixth of the globe. The revolutionary scientific ideas of Marx and Engels were put into practice. Leninism took shape as the logical development of Marxism in the age of imperialism. The workers and the exploited of the world established their first and firmest stronghold in the struggle for the revolutionary transfer of society, a powerful tool of science and ideology, an experience and an invaluable program for action."

[6] In his 26 July 1971 speech, Fidel Castro for the first time admitted having made errors during the course of the revolution.

[7] *The Economist*, 13 January 1973.

less direct methods of preservation and control: dependence, sovietization, and legitimization.

Cuba's reliance on Soviet military and economic aid is already well known. In addition, in 1972 the Soviet Union accounted for 47.9 percent of Cuban trade, and the Communist world as a whole took nearly 70 percent.[8] Another form of dependence has also evolved in the last decade. Originally the Cuban development strategy called for rapid industrialization. By 1964, the Soviet leaders had persuaded Castro that, in light of the "socialist division of labor," his country should concentrate on the production of sugar and nickel, which is exactly what Cuba had always done under capitalism. While the price for sugar in the Soviet-Cuban trade agreements was above the world price at the time, actual payment for the sugar came in the form of overpriced, inferior Soviet goods.[9] Any sugar left over after the needs of domestic and socialist-camp consumption had been met could be sold for hard cash in the Western world. This has meant that, because of short harvests or low prices, the Cubans have been heavily dependent on inferior Soviet imports, while remaining an export monoculture.[10]

Keeping Cuba Communist is not simply a matter of imposing discipline from outside. What counts ultimately is developing in Cuba a cadre committed to the Soviet world view. It is not coincidence that Cuba, once thought oddly out of place in the dour socialist world, in recent years has acquired an ideological coat of fresh gray paint. The present Cuban Communist party acquired that name in 1965, but only in the last five years has it gained in importance at the expense of *personalismo*.[11] Meanwhile, Cuban journals, *Granma* and *Verde Olivo* in particular, now devote articles to such subjects as the strengthening of party life in language lifted from the pages of *Kommunist* or *Partinaya Zhizn*.

More significantly, Cubans in apparently increasing numbers are being trained in higher party schools in the Soviet Union. At home,

[8] Morris Rothenberg, "Current Cuban-Soviet Relationships: The Challenge to U.S. Policy," Occasional Papers in International Affairs (Coral Gables, Fla.: Center for Advanced International Studies, University of Miami, 1974).

[9] Regarding the efficacy of Russian machinery, Fidel Castro once confessed to K. S. Karol that Soviet cane cutters were "a great destroyer—where it had passed nothing will grow for a long time to come." Quoted by Leon Gouré and Julian Weinkle, "Cuba's New Dependency," in Jaime Suchlicki, ed., Cuba, Castro, and Revolution (Coral Gables, Fla.: University of Miami Press, 1972), pp. 144-89.

[10] Ibid., pp. 157-78.

[11] There is, as yet, no hint that Cuba has been in the grip of the personality cult. Nor have the Soviets directly urged the Cubans on to collective leadership. But judging from the current literature such suggestions may be in the offing.

preparations are being made for the first party congress and full-scale Soviet-style elections in 1975.[12] Cuban leaders including Castro have reminded their audiences that the party alone is immortal—that is, capable of preserving the revolution over the long term.[13] These developments have been warmly applauded by the Soviet leaders.[14]

Another way of preserving the regime is to promote acceptance of it in the non-Communist world. As a Moscow radio commentator, Viktor Levin, said after Cuba and West Germany resumed relations in January 1975:

> In the first place, it affirms the strengthening of the international authority of Cuba: It is essential to realize that the agreement between Havana and Bonn has been reached at a time when the tendency to establish normal relations with Cuba is gathering strength. . . . Secondly, under these conditions the recognition of revolutionary Cuba by one of the biggest capitalist states, which by chance is situated in another part of the world, may play the role of a catalyst for this positive process.[15]

What the commentator left unsaid was that Bonn's decision might be imitated by the United States—an even bigger capitalist state. Moscow wants the United States to accept the permanence of the Cuban revolution, just as it recognized the Soviet state in 1933. Direct negotiations leading to resumed relations, which in turn would lead

---

12 *Washington Post*, 22 October 1974, p. 18; *Granma Weekly Review* (Havana), 20 October 1974, p. 10. The flavor of this sovietization can be gotten from the slogans issued after a meeting of party secretaries from Havana province: "We will advance toward the party's first congress more resolutely by raising revolutionary awareness"; "Strengthening the party means strengthening the revolution"; "Onward to the first party congress raising economic effectiveness to the utmost." Havana television, 7 December 1974, reported in *FBIS Daily Report, Latin America*, 8 December 1974.

13 See speech by Armando Hart, politburo member, to new party members in *Granma Weekly Review* (Havana), 22 December 1974, p. 4. See *FBIS Daily Report, Latin America*, 3 January 1975, for a list of party slogans for 1975.

14 See, for example, O. Darusenkov, "Cuba—USSR: Solid Friendship," *International Affairs* (Moscow), February 1974, especially pp. 19-20. The Soviets no doubt entertain a deep hope that Castro will step aside himself, and this perhaps found expression in Juan Marinello's statement that the revolution's chief as well as President Osvaldo Dorticós would resign before the 1976 elections. Marinello is an old Communist (PSP) whose loyalties are very much directed toward Moscow. Reported in *El Día* (Mexico City), 7 January 1975, p. 1.

15 Moscow Radio, 21 January 1975, reported in *FBIS Daily Report, Soviet Union*, 22 January 1975. Levin notes further that the Federal Republic broke relations in 1963 because Cuba had opened relations with East Germany. But Bonn's policy of isolating the G.D.R. turned out to be self-defeating: "it was the Federal Republic which was isolated. . . ."—an obvious parallel to U.S.-Cuban relations.

to some kind of open and solemn guarantee of Cuban sovereignty, is probably the scenario desired by the Soviet government.[16]

What the U.S.S.R. Hopes to Gain. But why should the Kremlin go to all this trouble? The Soviet Union sees possibly three advantages in keeping Cuba on the correct path.

Recently, Russian dissident Zhores Medvedev stated that Cuba was no longer of any strategic value to Moscow and that the U.S.S.R. would welcome the island's integration into the Western Hemisphere, which would relieve it of an onerous economic burden.[17] Medvedev is right, in a sense. The problem revolves around the meaning of "strategic." While it is true that Cuba is not an important link in Soviet strategy, it does have some value. There are several military benefits for the Soviet Union in having the "island of freedom" in the socialist camp. The first lies in its potential as a base for nuclear-missile-equipped submarines. It is one of the worst-kept secrets of the cold war that the Soviet Union began constructing a submarine base at Cienfuegos in the fall of 1970—a facility that could extend time on station for Soviet submarines by as much as 20 to 50 percent.[18] Although the construction of the facility was completed, strenuous U.S. objection to its use led to an extension of the 1962 agreement which forbade the servicing of "nuclear submarines." On 4 January 1971, President Nixon made public this new amendment and added:

> We are watching the situation closely. The Soviet Union is aware of the fact that we are watching closely. We expect them to abide by the understanding. I believe they will.
>
> I don't believe that they want a crisis in the Caribbean and I don't believe that one is going to occur, particularly since the understanding has been clearly laid out and has been so clearly relied on by us, as I stated here today.[19]

Since that agreement, Soviet policy has been to test its ambiguities. What precisely constitutes "servicing"? More important, what is a

---

[16] V. Matveyek, "Reasonable Appeals," *Izvestia*, 8 March 1974, p. 3. Also *Pravda*, 16 October 1974, p. 5, in a Tass report that quotes (with obvious approval) U.S. press criticism of current American policy.

[17] *Washington Star*, 9 October 1974.

[18] *U.S. News and World Report*, 12 October 1970, pp. 22-23.

[19] President Nixon, interview on NBC News, 4 January 1971 (mimeo), pp. 1-2. A month later, Nixon admitted to an ambiguity in the agreement when he acknowledged the difficulty of distinguishing between servicing and a port call. News conference, 17 February 1971, reprinted in *Department of State Bulletin*, 8 March 1971, p. 284.

"nuclear submarine"? Does that term include nuclear-powered vessels which carry only conventional weapons? Does it include diesel-powered craft equipped with nuclear missiles? Soviet submarines have continued to arrive at Cuban ports, including Cienfuegos, since the agreement. The type of submarine sent to Cuba has escalated in military significance, and so has the publicity surrounding each visit. The most serious probe of the agreement came in April 1974 with the visit of a Golf-class submarine—diesel-powered, but equipped with nuclear ballistic missiles—without protest from the United States.[20]

Valuable as increased Soviet strategic capability on Cuba would be, it is only one variable in the military equation. Cuba might equally become one corner of a "transatlantic triangle" (the others being Portugal and Guinea) from which the Soviet Union could effectively sweep the area with intelligence-gathering ships and planes and in wartime carry out massive destruction of Western shipping.[21]

The second advantage of a Soviet Cuba would be its use for espionage activities. Since 1967, Cuban foreign intelligence (the DGS) has been closely tied to the KGB. One direct benefit from all of this for the Russians is the ability to use Cubans for gathering information unavailable to any East European.[22] Cubans are also reported to be training guerrillas in Guinea and Angola and teaching Southern Yemenis the fine art of flying MiGs.[23]

The Cubans provide their Soviet ally one other advantage. Despite his taming, Fidel Castro retains his prestige as a great revolutionary leader. Moreover, he has been a useful friend to Moscow, helping secure the Soviet world's left flank, especially against the persistent Chinese charge of revisionism. With Castro expounding the revolutionary merit of Leonid Brezhnev, as he did at the Algiers conference, the Kremlin is more likely to be taken seriously in circles it sometimes has difficulty in reaching.

Cuba's New International Strategy

Fidel Castro's objective is survival. But his self-preservation does not coincide exactly with the Soviet goal. In fact, the Soviet leaders

---

[20] Barry Blechman and Stephanie Levinson, "U.S. Policy and Soviet Subs," *New York Times*, 22 October 1974.

[21] *Washington Star*, 1 February 1975, and *Washington Post*, 4 February 1975.

[22] In a story first published in *London Evening News*, 26 March 1973, a Cuban diplomatic defector reported that the Cubans were operating a spy ring for the Soviets in London. See also *Washington Post*, 27 March 1973.

[23] *Washington Post*, 25 June 1973 and 11 November 1975. Both Guinea and South Yemen, of course, are Soviet client states.

might be delighted if the Cuban chief were to vanish from the scene. The Kremlin's goal is keeping alive a regime dedicated to its version of Marxism-Leninism. A tropical Titoism, much less Maoism, would simply not do. The Cubans, however, can afford to be more flexible. Indeed, few are really dedicated to anything[24] except making revolution—which really meant breaking abruptly from the Cuban past.

Beyond self-preservation, there are no firm constraints on Cuban policy. In 1965 Fidel Castro believed that Cuba's mission was to spearhead a revolutionary movement throughout Latin America, and who knows after that? A decade later his policy has shifted to selective fraternization with some regimes in the region and low-key enmity with the others.

Why Fidel Castro changed his strategy is a simple question without a simple answer. The conventional one, namely, that Che Guevara's failure in Bolivia persuaded the Cuban leader that his ex-minister of industry's strategy was faulty, is not convincing. For one thing, Castro's actions (or, more precisely, his nonactions) in support of the Bolivian venture suggest that he never believed that it would succeed.[25] Moreover, the defeat of guerrilla movements in Venezuela and Peru and the American intervention in the Dominican Republic must have convinced Castro by 1965 that revolution Havana-style did not work. Yet both revolutionary rhetoric and limited support for subversion in Latin America continued until the early 1970s. Failure may have contributed to the change in policy, but two other factors were at least as important. First, the Kremlin began pressing for a more "pragmatic" and cautious approach to revolution, and—in order for their pressure to be effective—increasing Cuba's dependence on the Soviet Union. Second, and perhaps more important, the Cubans felt able to change when they knew that their own revolution was secure. Castro made clear in the first years of the revolution that Cuba could never be safe as the only "free territory" in the hemisphere. In recent years, Castro and his immediate entourage have expressed confidence and satisfaction in the success of the revolution. The counter-revolutionaries, the CIA, and their own mistakes have all been overcome.

How permanent the change in Cuban strategy will be is open to question. In the first place, it is a distortion to speak only of Cuban

---

[24] There are two clear and important exceptions to this generalization, Raul Castro and Carlos Rafael Rodrígues.

[25] For the closest scrutiny of Castro's behavior during this whole curious episode, see Léo Sauvage, *Che Guevara: The Failure of a Revolutionary* (Englewood Cliffs, N.J.: Prentice-Hall, 1973), pp. 91-122.

policy. Behind the smooth, polished surface of traditional international relations jargon is a volatile, ambitious leader who defies prediction.[26] Circumstances may have compelled Fidel Castro to trim here and there, but his deepest feelings are not likely to have changed. They merely remain in check until the moment is again favorable for old-fashioned, romantic revolution throughout the hemisphere.

Though a firm friend of the Soviet Union and its international line, Castro has not been an ardent admirer of "peaceful coexistence" in recent years. He is, at best, a late and reluctant supporter of this policy as well as its corollary, détente.[27] Not until Brezhnev's January 1974 visit to Havana did he officially endorse peaceful coexistence in a joint Cuban-Russian communiqué. Earlier, in Castro's welcoming speech, he had made only one favorable reference to détente (after a blistering attack on the United States) and the "peace policy" of the Soviet Union—which, according to sovietologists, is not the same thing as peaceful coexistence. Castro's long-standing reservations about peaceful coexistence are not difficult to fathom. By 1960 he had already assumed that the United States would be unalterably opposed to a "genuine revolution" and that the Soviet Union alone was ready and able to protect him. The thought of any collaboration between the superpowers aroused the fear of a Soviet sellout.[28] Hence, the fundamental irreconcilability of the two systems is in Cuba's interest.

Suspicion about détente, however, has not locked Castro into total reliance on the Soviet Union. In the last few years new efforts

---

[26] Any attempt to negotiate with Cuba requires a clear understanding of the fact that Fidel Castro remains a tough, clever, and ultimately ruthless opponent. Any denigration of him as a petty Caribbean tyrant misses the point almost completely. Petty tyrants, for one thing, do not bring the world to the edge of nuclear catastrophe nor amass a following of adoring disciples ready to risk their necks for the thinnest kind of ideological gruel; nor do they alternately baffle, irritate, alarm, please, intrigue, and defy the machinations of both superpowers—and survive.

[27] His first "friendly" reference to détente also contained what must be described as a Freudian slip. In his 26 July 1973 speech, after predicting the swift decline of the American empire, Castro added: "In the present conditions of criminal détente (Castro corrects himself) international détente, that criminal blockade appears evermore an unjust, ridiculous and untenable act in the eyes of the world." Radio Havana, 26 July 1973, reported in FBIS Daily Report, Latin America, 27 July 1973.

[28] Castro's fear is not unprecedented in the Communist world. Albania remained an ally of the Soviet Union until Khrushchev ended his country's cold war with Yugoslavia, Albania's mortal enemy. After six years of bickering, Moscow broke relations with Albania on 3 December 1961. Nicholas Pano, People's Republic of Albania (Baltimore: Johns Hopkins University Press, 1968), p. 156.

at finding political and economic allies have been made, and the search has not been confined to the Communist world. In fact, relations with China remain cool, and news of lesser regimes like North Korea and North Vietnam, once so warmly hailed by the Cuban press, has been consigned to the back pages of *Granma*. But this has decidedly not been the case with either Western Europe or Latin America. Recently, for example, Carlos Rafael Rodrígues, Havana's number three man, completed a visit to Europe—a mission which netted new economic agreements with France and Spain as well as renewed relations with West Germany. In addition, Cuba has been very actively cultivating friendship with Portugal.

Cuba in the Latin American Community. But it is Latin America that has received the closest attention since Castro announced on 26 July 1972:

> We are in this hemisphere, on this side of the Atlantic. We are Latin Americans. We know that no small country will have even the slightest chance of advancing in the world of tomorrow, which will be a world of great human and economic communities, with a gigantic scientific and technological revolution, in the midst of struggle against an imperialism that still exists and will continue to exist for a certain period of time. In the future we will be economically integrated with Latin America. Of course, we aren't going to be integrated with the United States, because of our differences in language, customs, ideas, and everything else, which are very great, in spite of the fact that we are internationalists. We think that one day we will be politically and economically integrated with the rest of the peoples of Latin America.[29]

To affirm Cuba's future participation in a Latin American community is not necessarily to abandon an overt revolutionary strategy in the region, but it is to place the emphasis elsewhere. The shift is partly the result of changes in Latin America itself.

Cubans now argue that by the late 1960s the region's previously docile regimes had begun challenging a weakened U.S. imperialism. Anti-Yankee defiance took many forms: nationalization of American investments, formation of Latin-only economic groups like the Andean Common Market, and in general, "the rise of nationalistic,

---

[29] Radio Havana, 26 July 1972, reported in *FBIS Daily Report, Latin America*, 27 July 1972.

anti-imperialist, and anti-oligarchic governments."[30] Sérgio Alpízar wrote in *Verde Olivo*, house organ of the Cuban armed forces (FAR):

> Despite their vacillations, [these regimes] were impelled, among other concurrent factors, by their increasing decapitalization and by the rising anti-imperialist and revolutionary liberation movement undertaken by vast labor, student and popular sectors—and even including groups from the middle classes and military patriots—motivated by the need for securing structural changes.[31]

There were difficulties, even reverses, like the overthrow of Bolivia's Juan José Torres in 1971 and Chile's Salvador Allende in 1973. But, Alpízar said, the "historic time will come when the dreams of Bolívar and Martí are a beautiful reality."

Cuba's new dialogue with Latin America is proceeding along two tracks. First, Cuba is encouraging and participating in the emergent Latin American community. Second, it is interacting bilaterally with a wide assortment of governments in the region, many of which it would have scorned or subverted only a decade ago. The multilateral tack itself has two aspects. First, Cuba continues to revile the OAS— in terms of abuse rivalled only by the epithets Castro has hurled at the United States.[32] This abuse is not just another quirk of the Cuban premier. It fits into a sophisticated calculation of self-interest. Since the OAS and its predecessors have always been sustained by the United States, such organizations can present few opportunities for a regime bent on a fundamental reordering of the hemisphere. Instead, Cuba's new multilateralism has drawn it into exclusively Latin groupings, such as OLADE, the Latin American energy organization.[33] Cuba has once more become part of the Latin caucus at the U.N., and its representatives have attended, among other things,

---

30 Sérgio P. Alpízar, *Verde Olivo* (Havana), 17 November 1974, pp. 14-18.

31 Ibid., p. 15.

32 During an interview with Panamanian newsmen in August 1974, Fidel Castro made his views about the OAS perfectly clear: "We have said clearly that we will not become members of the OAS again, because the OAS has been an instrument of imperialist domination in Latin America. . . . History shows us too many examples of the uselessness of the OAS and how the OAS has been an instrument of imperialist aggression against the countries of Latin America. We are in favor of an organization of Latin American countries and the English speaking countries of the Caribbean that will provide a true instrument for our peoples to deal with any kind of aggression." Radio Libertad (Panama City), 26 August 1974, reported in *FBIS Daily Report, Latin America*, 27 August 1974.

33 At OLADE's fourth meeting, Manuel de Céspedes, Cuba's minister of mines and metallurgy, was elected a vice-president of the organization. *Diario de las Americas* (Miami), 20 August 1974.

the Latin American-EEC meeting in Montevideo in March 1974 and the celebrations marking the anniversary of the Battle of Ayacucho (1825). Castro has announced his support for the Latin American Economic System (SELA) which would help member nations produce and market the region's raw materials at higher prices.[34]

The Cubans are enjoying even more success bilaterally. At first only certified anti-imperialist, pro-Marxist regimes (Allende's Chile or Torres's Bolivia) were treated as worthy of friendship with the "island of freedom." But then "nationalist" or "antioligarchic" governments like Velasco's Peru or Torrijos's Panama were invited into the charmed circle.[35] Then Venezuela's Carlos Andrés Pérez—who, as President Betancourt's minister of the interior, ran the campaign that liquidated pro-Castro guerrillas in the 1960s—was hailed for his defense of Venezuela's natural resources. "Venezuela will not be alone as long as the common struggle of the Latin American nations and the defenders of peace and progress exists," trumpeted a communiqué issued by the Cuban Movement for Peace and the Sovereignty of Nations, one of those instant "mass organizations," in November 1974.[36] Less than two months later, relations were restored between these once bitter enemies.[37] By early 1975, the Cubans were wooing even the conservative regimes in Colombia and Costa Rica—enjoying more success with the former than the latter.[38] Closer to home, Cuba has resumed commercial and diplomatic relations with the English-speaking Caribbean states, and even the conservative government of Joaquín Balaguer in Santo Domingo (a Cuban bête noire if there ever was one) has successfully initiated talks with Havana on protecting the price of sugar.[39]

The Meaning of Cuba's New Strategy. Cuba has not made a complete diplomatic turnabout. There remain governments it refuses to have anything to do with: most prominently Uruguay and Chile.

---

[34] Latin America (London), 13 December 1974; Washington Post, 4 January 1975.

[35] Relations with Argentina have cooled noticeably since Perón's death, but Castro has not openly denounced the new government, as he would have in the old days, for its swing to the right.

[36] Radio Havana, 25 November 1974, and reported in FBIS Daily Report, Latin America, 26 November 1974.

[37] Christian Science Monitor, 6 January 1975.

[38] Bogota Radio Cadena Nacional, 8 January 1975, and an AFP (Paris) report, 7 January 1975, and reported in FBIS Daily Report, Latin America, 13 January 1975.

[39] Santo Domingo Radio Clarín, 13 December 1974, and reported in FBIS Daily Report, Latin America, 14 December 1974.

Others, like Guatemala and El Salvador, reject rapprochement with Cuba for the moment, although Guatemala's President Kjell Laugerud refuses relations only "while Fidel Castro is there."[40] Nevertheless, the change in Cuban strategy is remarkable. The question remains: why the shift? And more important, what does it portend for the United States? Some explanations have already been suggested—the failure of the old policy and the development of new opportunities—and these the Cubans themselves have publicly acknowledged. In addition, there is no question that approaches to Venezuela and now Mexico are inspired by the hope of securing nearby oil supplies—a hope warmed by the prospect of increased Soviet prices for petroleum.[41]

Cuba's new approach to Latin America should not leave American policy makers complacent. The Second Declaration of Havana espousing guerrilla warfare may have been consigned to the dustbin of history for the moment, but the animus behind it has not been tempered.[42] The Cuban regime may be more dangerous to the United States now than when it supported isolated guerrilla bands whose only success was in frightening Latin American governments into cooperating (for once) with the United States.

In addition, Cuba has not completely given up on subversion. Both Chile and Uruguay have reported in detail Cuban assistance to local guerrilla groups. Cuba has also provided radio and television time to the Nicaraguan rebels who, through the use of hostages, managed to escape to Havana.[43] Moreover, the Cuban press has warmly endorsed the Puerto Rican extremists as well as the oldest

---

[40] LATIN news agency (Buenos Aires), 20 December 1974, and reported in FBIS Daily Report, Latin America, 21 December 1974.

[41] Washington Post, 29 January 1975. Castro's attempt to get oil below OPEC prices has so far not met with success—to his increasing annoyance.

[42] At the June 1975 meeting of the hemisphere's Communist parties—the first of its kind since November 1964—a communiqué was signed by all the parties that endorsed nearly all of Soviet foreign policy including a bitter attack on the People's Republic of China. However, while guerrilla action was not mentioned (much less endorsed), and unity of all "anti-imperialist forces" stressed—a clear slap at the sectarian fidelista groups of the 1960s—the documents all asserted the "right and duty of all popular and revolutionary forces to be ready to reply to counter-revolutionary violence with revolutionary violence—including armed struggle." Thus, the June meeting does continue the long-term trend of Castro's turning away from exclusive reliance on violent action in Latin America. But the formula for revolution is broad enough to permit armed action against those regimes (particularly in Chile and Uruguay) that the Cuban leader especially detests. See Latin American Topics, July 1975.

[43] Radio Havana (international service), 3 January 1975, reported in FBIS Daily Report, Latin America, 4 January 1975.

functioning guerrilla band in the region—the so-called Army of National Liberation (ELN) in Colombia.[44] Finally, Havana has not yet denounced such terrorist groups as the Argentine ERP, even though Moscow has done so. Such activity is pursued at a lower level and far more discreetly than it was in the early 1960s, but it does continue. Increasingly Cuba's policy has resembled the traditional two-track approach of the Soviet Union: encouragement of conventional relations on the one hand, supplemented by more or less discreet subversion on the other.

If Castro is still pursuing an anti-American strategy, albeit with a shift in tactics, why should he engage in talks with the United States? Some answers have already been suggested: for example, the Cubans are under pressure from Moscow. But Castro has his own reasons for wanting talks. Lifting the embargo would be highly desirable. Castro has made no secret of the damage it has done or the Russians' inability to fill the gap with their own inferior goods. Moreover, Cuba is as eager to get American technology as the rest of the socialist camp.

One more factor needs consideration, and that is the present mood of the Cubans, especially Castro. Only last year when sugar prices were rising Castro expressed confidence that the United States would have to talk with him in order to secure a reasonably priced supply of sugar. With the recent swift decline in sugar prices and Cuban difficulties in meeting a mediocre goal of 6 million tons, that rosy optimism has faded. Nevertheless, recent American reverses in Indochina coupled with the energy crisis and the recession have reinforced Castro's conviction that the United States is entering an era of swift and permanent decline. Weakened, distracted, and internally divided, as the Cuban leaders see it, the United States also faces growing difficulties with Latin America, which are only aggravated by its poor relations with Cuba. For all of these reasons, Castro undoubtedly believes the time is ripe for tough negotiations leading to significant concessions from the United States.

United States Strategy

In the light of Soviet and Cuban aims, how should this country act in the coming months and perhaps years in dealing with Cuba? To discuss a new American policy we must be precise about our objectives.

---

[44] *Granma Weekly Review* (Havana), 5 July 1974.

Our Long-term Objectives. The long-term goal for the United States can be no less than the ending of the Marxist-Leninist regime in Cuba without resort to war, subversion, or even embargo. It must be stressed that this is the ultimate aim of the United States, just as the fall of capitalist America is the ultimate aim of the Cuban regime. Neither side should expect its goal to be reached soon, or even within two or three decades.

But why in this age of détente, of ideological pluralism, should that be our aim? And how practical is it? Where has a Communist regime been overthrown by peaceful means? If this is our goal for Cuba, why is it not our goal for the whole Communist world? Obsoleteness, impracticality, and inconsistency, in short, are the objections raised to this objective.

The charge of obsoleteness is irrelevant when it is rooted in a misunderstanding of the nature of détente. Détente is based on a mutual desire to avoid war and reduce the cost of military preparedness. It does *not* aspire to ending the competition between the capitalist and Communist systems, which, for all the talk of convergence, are still widely divergent in both political principle and performance. There is a vital point, after all, to the competition as it is understood by serious men on both sides: the ultimate victory, even if only in the distant future, of their most deeply held beliefs. The case of Cuba only underlines the point. Cuban Marxism-Leninism is an especially flammable fuel, combining as it does the most extreme form of Cuban nationalism with a primitive Leninism that has not yet been neutralized by cynicism or experience or disappointment.

The charge of impracticality carries more weight. Western success in rolling back communism has not been merely limited, it has been nonexistent. Nevertheless, Cuba is a kind of test case for the United States as an abiding alternative to tyranny. The largest and sturdiest of police states, the Soviet Union, still resists the intrusion of the Western world in the form of the press, films, literature, and the freely roaming tourist. There is very little evidence to suggest that this concern is not justified. But if a hugely complex and remote hermit kingdom equipped with an efficient secret police can rightly fear cautious, peaceful Western penetration, how much more a tiny neighboring police state has to worry about—and how much more likely peaceful subversion is to succeed. The goal *is* feasible (and might actually be pursued, especially after the passing of Fidel Castro) if we are clear about our aim and tenacious and patient in its pursuit.

As for inconsistency, it is true we are concerned about making Cuba, rather than the Soviet Union or China, socialism's first apostate, because Cuba presents us with an exceptional opportunity. Moreover, it is a strange doctrine which states that Havana must be treated exactly like Moscow or Peking, coming as it does from the very school of political theology which only a few years ago belabored the thesis that the Communist world was no longer a monolith. Indeed, it is not, and should not be dealt with as if it were.

Our Short-term Goals. Our long-range goal, admirable as it is (especially in a time of American retreat), must be supplemented with short-term objectives. In other words, what will our Cuba policy look like for the next few years? The following suggestion is not original, but it is worth considering: namely, our short-term goal should be the severing of the Moscow connection.

Let us be precise about this. For the moment, it is out of the question that the Cuban regime might stop looking toward the Soviet Union for ideological sustenance and economic-military aid, and there is little that can be done about this. Furthermore, the Soviet Union remains an almost ideal ally for the distant small power. Over the last fifteen years it has proven a faithful one as well—except possibly during the October missile crisis. Unlike the United States, the Soviet Union has stood by its small, exposed ally at heavy economic cost to itself with little in the way of public complaint, and there is no evidence that it will change.[45]

But Cuba *can* be eliminated as a forward military base for our leading adversary—and this objective is deeply rooted in the history of American foreign policy. Furthermore, it falls within the parameters of détente. Détente cannot possibly be significant to both sides if the Kremlin makes the Caribbean an area of major naval deployment. Our insistence on the Caribbean as a Soviet-free zone should not be interpreted by anyone as a peremptory military threat to Cuba. The United States has never even considered using its own forces to invade Cuba since the inception of the Castro regime, except at the height of the missile crisis. In the dozen years since then there is no evidence that American policy makers have ever entertained the possibility. Furthermore, the Cubans have never been protected directly by Soviet armed forces, but have relied instead on their own considerable military strength and U.S. self-restraint.

---

[45] Some would argue that the United States had no formal defense treaty with South Vietnam (much less Cambodia), and therefore that American withdrawal was not an act of faithlessness. Yet the Soviet Union has no formal agreement with the Cubans either—it has persistently refused Cuba admission to the Warsaw Pact—and yet the Castro regime has thrived largely thanks to Soviet support. We need to be more than black letter lawyers in coping with the delicate nuances of security and survival in the present day world.

The Three Levels of American Policy. Defining objectives, of course, is one thing and bringing them about is another. American strategy should operate on three levels: multilateral, trilateral, and bilateral. As for the first, the United States must begin to take seriously the prospect of an increasingly alienated Latin America prodded on by Cuba, eager to lead, within the region's councils. Considering the responsive chord it has already struck from such diverse regimes as Peru and Venezuela, Cuba could well be more harmful to this country as a promoter of anti-Americanism among established Latin governments in the mid-1970s than it ever was in the early 1960s as a promoter of guerrilla warfare *against* established Latin governments.

A sound policy for Latin America would neither patronize nor demean these countries. Neither would it involve large sums of money. And it is possible, provided American leaders stop assuming that a pious formula thought up by the latest Latin American study commission *is* a policy. On the other hand, the Cubans should never be encouraged in the belief that anything goes short of outright subversion or, worse, that mere truculence will win them concessions from us.

There are certain issues that must involve the Soviet Union as well as Cuba. Those, however, should be kept to an absolute minimum. Excessive deference to Soviet "interests" simply legitimizes the Russian position in Cuba—which directly conflicts with our fundamental objective in the Caribbean. If we are not prepared to insist on a minimalist role for the Soviet Union in an area considered by us for the last two centuries as vital, then we are not likely to be taken seriously on any of the other issues that still divide East and West.

One matter involving all three parties is the future of Guantánamo.[46] Although surrender of the base to Cuba is no longer one of Castro's conditions for beginning talks, the issue must eventually be faced, and the later the better. There are good arguments for preserving Guantánamo as a U.S. facility since we hold it in perpetuity.[47] The Cuban government has no legal case and it has not bothered to test its brief in any judicial forum. Nevertheless, Guantánamo will probably be turned over to Cuba—a gratifying development for Cuban nationalism. Under no circumstances can those facilities then be made available to the Kremlin. An agreement must

---

[46] Negotiations with the Soviet Union on the issue of its naval craft using Cuban facilities should be bilateral in scope.

[47] One of them is the prohibitive cost of replacement—an unlikely event especially in an era of congressional constraint on defense spending.

be worked out forbidding this eventuality, although, despite solemn assurances, the Soviet Union might test such an agreement. In that case, the United States must be prepared to take previously announced limited military actions to stop any violation of a new Guantánamo treaty.

Our Bilateral Policy: Negotiations

The most sensitive and difficult area of our policy will be the talks with the Cubans themselves. Even starting them will not be easy, for there is much that divides our two countries, and, despite appearances, each government remains uncertain at the highest levels about what the other's intentions really are.

Ending the Embargo. At least two prenegotiation steps must be taken. During a period of continued probing and testing of one another's hopes and expectations, very private talks between middle-level officials from both sides will probably take place. (Throughout this phase, highly publicized trips by self-starting congressmen, journalists, and presidential candidates who have no clearer idea of what the State Department is up to than does Fidel Castro should be avoided. These "fact-finding" missions find no new facts, inflate expectations, beg Cuban manipulation, and sustain the illusion that the United States will be in a desperate fix if it does not deal with Havana immediately.) But even preliminary discussions cannot begin until the matter of the economic sanctions has been settled through the OAS. Not to formally rescind the sanctions would further weaken an already sickly organization—and one does not have to be an extreme admirer of multilateral diplomacy to realize that a moribund OAS would be a positive development for Cuba.[48] If the OAS should dissolve, new regional arrangements would evolve—few of which would be to our liking. This consideration was overlooked by those who argued that the United States, like a number of Latin states, should ignore the sanctions and initiate talks with the Cubans to avoid becoming "isolated in the hemisphere."[49]

The attempt to remove the sanctions at the Quito meeting failed. The American abstention and failure to exercise leadership on either

---

[48] A decade ago the potential of the OAS was in danger of being vastly overrated by men who had uncritically accepted historicist notions about the world's progress from nation-states to regional communities. In the mid-1970s, these regionalist groupings are receiving the opposite (equally thoughtless) evaluation.
[49] It is interesting to note that such evaluations that appeared in the American press were soon followed by a similar conclusion on the part of Castro—an ardent consumer of U.S. media.

side of the question prompted the criticism from Latin America that the United States had acted in a patronizing manner. Though the meeting of the foreign ministers embarrassed the Venezuelans and Peruvians, the failure to end the sanctions caused this country little real damage. In December 1974 a new voting formula was proposed which would determine the fate of the sanctions by simple majority vote; it was adopted and, at the meeting in San José, Costa Rica, in July 1975, the sanctions were removed. In the meantime the delay has helped this country. Six months ago the Cubans were buoyed up by fresh waves of Latin resentment against the United States on the Cuba issue, and their extreme confidence would have made talks at that time all the more difficult.

OAS repeal did not of itself end the American embargo. This can be done only by an executive order rescinding the Treasury Department's Cuban Assets Control Regulations.[50] For these steps to be taken without corresponding concessions from the other side, of course, would involve great risk for the United States. But those who see our coming negotiations as operating on a strictly quid pro quo basis should know by now that there are many more American quids than Cuban quos: the relationship between the two countries is fundamentally asymmetrical. Furthermore, the termination of the embargo would not give Cuba free access to the American market.

Even aside from a new sugar quota (under Section 620 A of the Foreign Assistance Act, Congress cannot restore the Cuban quota until confiscated American property is paid for), two principal economic incentives would still be available to U.S. negotiators. The first involves most-favored-nation status (MFN) and the second is Cuba's eligibility for the generalized system of preferences (GSPs). The lifting of the embargo does not, of course, qualify Cuba for non-discriminatory treatment in trade matters. To qualify for most-favored-nation status, a bilateral commercial agreement must be negotiated, and under the new U.S. trade law (Section 405b) that agreement can last only three years and is renewable if:

> (A) a satisfactory balance of concessions in trade and services has been maintained during the life of such agreement, and
>
> (B) the President determines that actual or foreseeable reductions in United States tariffs and nontariff barriers to trade resulting from multilateral negotiations are satisfac-

---

[50] *Foreign Assets Control: Cuban Census Regulations and Forms under the Cuban Assets Control Regulations* (Washington, D.C.: Treasury Department, 31 January 1964).

torily reciprocated by the other party to the bilateral agreement.[51]

Any such treaty may be suspended "at any time for national security reasons," and the agreement can only go into effect when approved by the Congress through the adoption of a concurrent resolution.[52] Aside from these rather general provisions, one very large barrier still remains: the provision for freedom of emigration within the Trade Act of 1974. It was Congress's clear intent to single out the Soviet Union on this matter, but the law, in fact, refers to all non-market economies, a description that fits Cuba exactly. Thus, in Sections 402 and 409 of the Trade Act, Cuba cannot qualify for the MFN or receive credits or credit guarantees if it:

(1) denies its citizens the right or opportunity to join permanently through emigration, a very close relative in the United States, such as a spouse, parent, child, brother, or sister;

(2) imposes more than a nominal tax on the visas or other documents required for emigration described in paragraph (1); or

(3) imposes more than a nominal tax, levy, fine, fee, or other charge on any citizen to emigrate as described in paragraph (1).[53]

Even if the Cuban government were to alter its present emigration policy (in the past when it did allow people to leave, it violated all three provisions of Section 409a), the MFN still cannot go into effect until the president submits a report to Congress detailing Cuban compliance and the Congress refrains from passing a resolution of disapproval within ninety days.[54]

Qualifying for the GSPs will be even more difficult for Cuba. However, unlike the developed Communist countries—Czechoslovakia, East Germany, Hungary, Poland, and the Soviet Union—Cuba is not excluded by name from the generalized system of preferences. As a Communist country, it must satisfy a long list of conditions. First, it must already be a trading partner in good standing. Second, it must be a member of the General Agreement on Tariffs and Trade (GATT) and the International Monetary Fund (IMF).[55] Third, it

---

[51] Trade Act of 1974, P.L. 93-618, 3 January 1975, p. 84.

[52] Ibid., pp. 84-85.

[53] Ibid., p. 85.

[54] Ibid.

[55] Cuba at present holds membership only in the GATT.

cannot be "dominated or controlled by international communism." Fourth, it must provide "prompt, adequate, and effective compensation" for "nationalized, expropriated, or otherwise seized . . . property owned by a United States citizen or by a corporation. . . ." The third and fourth requirements, naturally, will prove the most problematic for the Cubans, and will provide the United States with some leverage to use in prying the Cubans away from the Soviets. It is also quite likely that the Cubans will find these requirements so distasteful that they will forgo the advantages of the GSPs. However, as Cuba's economy begins to perk up in the next few years, the temptation to enter the nearby American market, especially with its new line of manufactured goods, might prove irresistible.

Despite this formidable array of incentives, the United States must be prepared for a long period of very hard bargaining. But the tools for effective negotiating are there. They need only be used.

Our Negotiating Goals. The principal purpose of the coming negotiations is to advance our short- and long-range goals. To assume that the purpose is to clear up past misunderstandings or to advance the cause of détente or to make policy toward the Communist world consistent would imply that negotiations with Albania might be as meaningful as talks with Cuba.[56] To advance our true goal, the United States must help end Cuba's isolation from the Western world. That isolation is apparent even from a quick look at the Cuban press. There is an almost endless stream of visiting Russian and East European officials as well as a small number of Latin American and third world guests. But the sum total of Western Europeans, Japanese, Canadians, and Americans remains tiny to this day.

---

[56] It is no inconsistency to deal with major Communist powers like the Soviet Union or the People's Republic while remaining aloof to the small people's republics (North Korea, North Vietnam, Albania, and Cuba). The first must be dealt with on some level, while the others remain inconsequential and obnoxious. Those who believe that Cuba has relaxed its hostility might consider this one small, and by no means untypical, news item from *Granma Weekly Review*, (Havana), 6 December 1974, p. 6. "Santiago Alvarez, deputy director of the ICAIC [Cuban Institute of Cinema Arts] has proposed that every socialist country prepare six film documentaries in which the acts of aggression committed by the United States since its establishment as a nation down to the present time are denounced. During his speech in a symposium on motion pictures held in Berlin, GDR, he pointed out that the bicentennial of the independence of the United States will be held in two years and he stated that socialist motion picture producers must take advantage of the opportunity to reflect those 200 years of violence." One wonders what kind of reaction an American film maker would get if he proposed that each major Western film studio make a series of anti-Communist movies.

How do we begin penetrating the sugar cane curtain? The task, while difficult, is not yet impossible. Cuba was a highly if imperfectly westernized country by 1959, more similar to Czechoslovakia than Bulgaria. The analogy is important because it was the Czechs in 1968 who nearly reverted to their democratic ways. That brings us to another point. Unlike Prague, Havana does not happen to lie on a principal tank route of the Warsaw Pact. To reestablish a Western presence in Cuba,[57] we must encourage two-way tourism, the reunion of Cubans now separated by the Florida Straits, and a reduction of bureaucratic restrictions on trade. Aid and investment are out for the time being, but surely educational opportunities might be provided for young Cubans in this country, even on a limited basis. Much of this cannot be done right away, and there will be much official Cuban fear of "cultural imperialism," but the new Soviet culture that is being pressed upon the Cuban people, especially the young, is even more inappropriate. Thus, American encouragement, under the right circumstances, of Cuba's integration within its true cultural family, Latin America, should also be part of the process.

Besides the main business of opening Cuba up to the non-Communist world, three issues are of immediate interest to us, and at least one of them can be related to our ultimate objective. They are political prisoners, U.S. private property claims, and Cuba's ambitious nuclear program. Of these, the political prisoner question should receive priority treatment.

How many political prisoners are there? Estimates vary widely since the Cuban government withholds the figures and refuses access to them by any outside group. The number may be as high as 60,000, but even 10,000 (a figure Castro has indirectly acknowledged) would be equivalent to nearly a quarter of a million in this country.[58]

For that matter, why should it concern us? This is clearly an internal matter and except for the controversial concern we have shown for Soviet Jewish emigrants (not Soviet political prisoners),

---

[57] The Cubans, of course, will be openly suspicious of this presence and demand the closest kind of restrictions, as the Soviets have. However, since nothing like grand strategic questions are at stake, this country can be especially insistent on this point since the Cubans so obviously need the economic help the technologically backward Soviet Union cannot provide. Moreover, this should not be viewed by the Cuban regime as any great concession since it is so sincerely convinced of socialism's superiority as a way of life.

[58] Sixty-thousand is the figure claimed by Juan Fernandez Pellicer in *El Universal* (Caracas), 20 March 1974; 40,000 is the figure usually advanced by the Cuban exile groups in this country; 10,000 is the number indirectly admitted to by Castro. See *Diario de las Americas* (Miami), 30 October 1974, and Terri Shaw, *Washington Post*, 1 June 1975.

there is no real precedent in our relations with Communist countries on this sensitive issue. But perhaps there should have been. We have demonstrated great concern for political prisoners much farther from home than Cuba. Brazil, Chile, Greece, and formerly South Vietnam come to mind. Aside from humanitarian concern, there is also a legitimate American interest at stake. An unknown but probably large number of U.S. citizens have friends and relatives in Cuban jails and they do not have the slightest indication of whether or not these prisoners are alive or when they will be released. Surely, as a first step this country can insist upon receiving a list of the living and dead. From that beginning we can press the "island of freedom" to be as forthcoming about its political prisoners as, say, the much despised Chilean regime has proved to be.

As for the U.S. property claims, the Foreign Claims Settlement Commission has certified 5,911 property loss claims amounting to $1.8 billion, filed by corporations and private citizens, from a total of 8,000 claims totalling $3.0 billion.[59] Of course, the commission did not reimburse anyone; it merely established which claims the U.S. government must pursue. A question remains: why should the United States, aside from legal obligations, take this issue so seriously? The corporations have long since written off their confiscated property as a tax loss. Why then bring it up in a period of warming relations, especially when American investment was a leading cause of the split in the first place?

This argument is not to be dismissed out of hand. It does have political merit and should be considered by American negotiators. Yet it is deficient for three reasons. First, it is not true that the claims all come from corporations. Individuals have been certified for over $220 million in losses, and 4,547 of them have claims of $50,000 or less. These claimants have not been eligible for tax loss write-offs —unlike the largest investors.[60] Second, the larger corporations may have cut their losses, but that does not mean no one has lost anything. In fact, it is the U.S. taxpayer who has made good the government's loss of corporate revenue. Third, there is a principle at stake here which is very much worth defending, although most of us have been long exposed to arguments demonstrating the ease with which we can bear the misfortunes of others. The situation is this: Americans

---

[59] Dana L. Thomas, "Castro Convertibles?" *Barron's*, 22 January 1973.

[60] Indeed, while the assertion is made that large corporations have been successful in recouping their losses through the tax law, even the extent of this is not known. See Lynn Darrell Bender, "U.S. Claims against the Cuban Government: An Obstacle to Rapprochement," *Inter-American Economic Affairs*, Summer 1973, p. 10.

have been plundered by a band of men who seized power by force and then found themselves uncertain as to what they were about. And plunder—the art of taking what belongs to another by force or fraud—is the precise word for the Cuban regime's "revolutionary" acts of 1959–1960. These acts violated international law. They contravened existing Cuban law. They went against the decree of the new regime itself.[61] The United States, then, should pursue the claims of its citizens with vigor. If it is lukewarm here, it will never be taken seriously in other cases where the merits are much less clear-cut. And even here, skill, patience, and persistence are called for on the part of the negotiators. Any solution will come only after protracted negotiations.

The last issue will have to be faced within the next five years. Cuba's nuclear power program was announced by Fidel Castro on 4 December 1974 in a Builders Day commemoration speech:

> We are now building thermoelectric plants, and in the next five-year period we will have to start building the first nuclear plant. The first nuclear plant will be started in 1977 or 1978 with a capacity of 440,000 kilowatts. That will be the first one. A second one is scheduled for the following five-year period, 1980 to 1985.
>
> But construction must be started in a few years because these are very complex constructions. All the required mechanical and chemical plants must be built.[62]

The Cubans will be assisted by the Soviet Union in this undertaking. Five days after Castro's startling announcement, Mikolay Maltsev, identified by Radio Havana as a "deputy minister for power and electrification," announced in Moscow his country's support for a Cuban nuclear program to consist of two 400- or 500-megawatt power reactors.[63]

It is likely that these reactors will be of the light water type capable of producing 200 to 300 kilograms of plutonium per year (assuming a capacity of 1,000 megawatts). This in itself represents no direct military capacity. Light water reactors are less suitable for weapons programs than heavy water reactors. They produce half the

---

[61] The new regime decreed that seized property would be paid for with twenty-year national bonds carrying a 4.5 percent interest rate. The bonds were never even issued.

[62] Radio Havana, 5 December 1974, reported in *FBIS Daily Report, Latin America*, 6 December 1974. See also *Times of the Americas* (New York), 25 December 1974.

[63] Radio Havana, 10 December 1974, reported in *FBIS Daily Report, Latin America*, 11 December 1974.

plutonium and are not designed for easy materials diversion. The Cubans, too, must fill in some gaps in the fuel cycle before they can fashion atom bombs. And filling these gaps will require Soviet help over the next decade. Two questions, then, are pertinent: will they do it? And if they do, does a nuclear Cuba represent any special danger to the United States?

No one in this country can answer the first question, but in the light of past relations and Fidel Castro's special character, the second must be answered in the affirmative. This would make necessary discussion of the matter on a trilateral basis. The best solution would be a negotiated Soviet withdrawal from Cuba's atomic program. Cuba, however, is deficient in fossil fuel, and a nuclear power program probably makes sense. The United States should consider sponsoring a safeguard assistance program, or at least encourage the International Atomic Energy Agency to lend a hand. Anything less will be difficult to monitor, much less control. The second-best solution would be a negotiated agreement with the Soviet Union guaranteeing that gaps in Cuba's nuclear fuel cycle will remain. Finally, a successful energy program without military potential could have one advantage for the Cubans that fits in with American objectives: it would reduce the island's dependence on Soviet oil— most certainly a precondition for any break with the socialist camp.

Cuba's Third Option

Even assuming that negotiations on these issues are concluded successfully, is there any chance that relations can go beyond the controlled hostility that seems the most likely possibility at this time?

To be very optimistic about relations with Cuba is to look at reality in a fun-house mirror. No matter how reasonable and accommodating U.S. officials may be, the initiative lies with the Cubans. In considering their future the Cubans must come to terms with the fact that they, like the Canadians and the Mexicans, must live next to the "world's most powerful and dynamic nation, the United States." [64] There is little likelihood that the United States will decline permanently, despite the dearest wishes of some Communist chieftains.

The Cubans have three options concerning the United States. First, Cuba may continue to be our enemy, maintaining a minimum of contact with the United States and remaining dependent on the Soviet Union. Second, Cuba could resume its past relationship with

---

[64] Quoted in Mitchell Sharp, "Canada-U.S. Relations: Options for the Future," *International Perspective* (Ottawa), Autumn 1972, p. 1.

America and become once more dependent on it for aid, trade, and investment. Third, the Cubans could choose to resume good relations with this country, and at the same time maintain a healthy variety of economic and political relationships with nations around the world. This last option is practical and violates the self-interest of neither side. Let us reiterate: no small power ever had an easy time of living next to a powerful neighbor. No small power, however, has had an easier time of it than Cuba. If this seems hard to accept, the Cuban leadership might ask the Czechs, the Latvians, the Mongolians, the Nepalese, or the Irish what their experience has been.

Time is running out on that kind of option. Cuba is being steadily sovietized as a stream of fresh Cuban apparatchiki return from Soviet party schools. By the time a few more years have gone by it will take a mighty change in direction to bring about good relations with the United States, and the only man capable of reorienting the regime now is Fidel Castro. He alone has the freedom of choice or even the intelligence to free himself from the narrow ideological straitjacket his contemporaries have so willingly accepted. Furthermore, Castro himself is only now in a position to contemplate a serious change in Cuban foreign policy. Whatever his failures in economics or misadventures in Latin America, he has accomplished a great task achieved by no other Cuban leader: he has molded his people into a nation. Now, unfortunately, he faces the prospect of debasing even this success as Cuba becomes more and more like a tropical Bulgaria. The direction is obvious and it should not be welcome to Cubans or Americans.

Even if that trend is altered, relations between these neighbors will never be free of problems. Geography and history make that impossible. But the problems can be dealt with and perhaps in part resolved. In the nineteenth century Americans fought and died for Cuban freedom—a fact still recognized in the Cuban press. Furthermore, American mistakes and shortcomings in this century do not merit the enmity generated by a philosophy which is foreign to the best in both the American and Cuban traditions. This is what American officials must reaffirm and Cuban leaders learn—perhaps for the first time.

Projections for the Coming Months

Most observers believe that the coming talks between the United States and Cuba will be long and arduous. Judging by the deep differences created by history and geography, such a prediction is hardly rash. But it does not tell us much.

It is important to go beyond this assertion and ask why the negotiations will be so difficult aside from the problems already discussed. For one thing, Cuban negotiating strategy will have two aspects. In private talks Cuban officials will remain firm if not intransigent in their demands. Publicly, however, they will probably insist that it is American stubbornness that prevents real progress, and thus appeal to groups in this country predisposed to be sympathetic to Cuba—which, as a small power, has the advantage of being an automatic underdog. The Cubans would probably hope that such an appeal would be effective with influential members of Congress, especially the Senate, the press, and the academy. The latter, it would also be hoped, would help create a climate of opinion that would place pressure on American negotiators.[65]

Thus, U.S. officials must be prepared for a well-designed and executed propaganda campaign that may hinder efforts to create a reasonable basis for economic and political relations. Meanwhile, those who are prone to accept the Cuban case must investigate the issues first and then decide who is being truly intransigent about what. The American press in particular has an important role to play in the coming negotiations. Its record in reporting Cuban developments has never been good. U.S. journalists (who, of course, are not alone in their ineptitude) have not done their job by settling for carefully guided tours of the island and relaying little more than the propaganda themes of the regime. Reporters must accept the plain fact that little hard news can be gathered on quick trips by first-time visitors who known little about the country and understand little or no Spanish.

---

[65] Very recently Cuba has been profiting from the negative picture of American intelligence services, especially the CIA, being developed by the media. Stories from various Cuban sources *now* reveal that some 100 assassination attempts have been made on the life of Fidel Castro and possibly other senior officials and that these attempts may still be going on today. The allegations deserve examination, though certainly not casual acceptance. First, the timing of their disclosure makes them automatically suspect. The Cuban government had fifteen years to make this generally known, but only now has it chosen to do so. Second, the details from the reports are contradictory: for example, there is confusion over the degree of CIA responsibility, the exact time period of the attempts, and the number of potential victims. Third, such spectacular failure on the part of a determined enemy also invites skepticism. Finally, it may be presumed that some if not most of the failed assassins were caught and tried or at least disposed of in some less formal manner. Yet there has been no record of such proceedings —the Cuban media have never mentioned any to the author's knowledge. A reasonable conclusion is that these charges are vastly inflated, baldly self-serving, and crudely opportunistic, and that a good deal more of the same can be expected from the Cuban regime in the future.

Journalists could follow events in Cuba more closely—the material available is nearly overwhelming—so as to more accurately reflect the current state of Cuban policy toward the United States as well as toward the Soviet Union. There is no reason, for example, why Fidel Castro's major speeches cannot be analyzed as thoroughly as his recent carefully staged press conferences with the American press have been. No single quotation from the Cuban leader will ever convey his intentions toward this country, especially when it is aimed primarily at an American audience. It is vital that the press look at statements made for other audiences: Latin American, Soviet, third world, and, of course, Cuban.

Whether these talks will lead to agreement on the larger issues (the Soviet military tie, Guantánamo, political prisoners) remains very much in doubt. Negotiations, especially if the United States has little left to bargain with, could become prolonged, bitter, and fruitless. What's more, political, like meteorological long-range forecasting is, at best, informed speculation. This projection, therefore, is not intended to anticipate every sudden change in the political climate. Indeed, if it fails to anticipate no more than a few diplomatic squalls, it may seem in retrospect more like science than art.

U.S.-Cuban negotiations could not begin, of course, until the OAS acted, which it did in San José, Costa Rica. Briefly, the foreign ministers amended the Rio Treaty to permit the ending of sanctions through a simple majority (member states must, however, still ratify this amendment), and they voted by a two-thirds majority to permit member states to deal with Cuba as they saw fit. Now that the sanctions are lifted, the United States is free to talk with the Cubans more or less in the open. But there will be at least several months of testing and probing by both sides during the first quarter of 1976.[66] This period will continue to be marked by more "gestures" from both sides; the United States, in particular, may well consider a partial lifting of the embargo (food and medicine, for example) in expecta-

---

[66] A recent good example of this was Fidel Castro's return of some $2 million in ransom money taken out of the United States by three desperados who commandeered a Southern Airways jet in 1972. The American response is instructive. Senator Sparkman, chairman of the Foreign Relations Committee, warmly praised the action and urged the administration to begin "a staged removal" of the trade embargo. The White House, on the other hand, was more circumspect. President Ford through another voice (Ron Nessen, press secretary) stated that the move was a "welcome development," but made no further comment. It may well have occurred to administration officials that proper procedure on the part of the Cuban government would have been a more prompt return of the loot. See the *New York Times*, 12 August 1975, and the *Washington Post*, 13 August 1975.

tion of an equally important Cuban signal (such as word on key political prisoners). But American negotiators should not be surprised if the Cubans instead give nothing, while holding out for an evisceration of U.S. trade regulations.

In the meantime, the value of "ping pong diplomacy" is vastly overrated. Unlike China, Cuba is not steeped in ignorance of the outside world. In fact, its leaders (who, of course, will determine their conduct during the negotiations without reference to the Cuban people) know America quite well, despite their insistence on wearing ideological glasses that color the United States in the most lurid shades.[67]

Once these preliminaries are over, discussions to establish consular offices to handle the limited trade and travel that will spring up may begin by midyear. After that, negotiations may well begin on the resumption of diplomatic relations, with serious argument perhaps arising over the size of each embassy's staff along with all the rules governing their freedom of movement. Judging by the difficulties encountered on these points by the Latin American countries that have decided to resume relations with Cuba, this will probably take a minimum of six months.

Thus, it is quite likely that negotiations on the issues will not begin until early 1977. Of course, even this schedule may be drawn out further if the Cubans expect a change of administration in the United States. From the American point of view, it may be well worth considering the use of multiple negotiating teams in Washington and Havana working on the separate issues that divide us. The progress of these teams would, of course, be monitored (along with Cuban actions in places like Latin America) by experts within the secretary of state's office. In this fashion, movement on the Guantánamo issue would be coordinated with progress in reducing the Soviet military connection. This approach would make it even more likely that negotiations would drag out over a long period of time. But this is not to be feared. The United States is not threatened by dire consequences if talks do not pay off immediately. Negotiating with Cuba is not analogous with reaching a settlement in the Middle East, and impatience for "concrete results" would be foolish. Even more foolish would be the expectation that things will go smoothly and that all

---

[67] There is some evidence to suggest that the view of the United States projected by the official Cuban media is not completely shared by the leadership, and Fidel Castro in particular. Under questioning by an American journalist in 1966, Fidel Castro did admit that his radio, television, and press distorted the news from America for political purposes. See Lockwood, *Castro's Cuba, Cuba's Fidel*, pp. 128-29.

problems ancient and modern will be somehow resolved. At best, the United States will only reverse its policy of isolating Cuba and begin the long process of tempting Cuba back from the neo-Stalinist society its leaders are now busily constructing. Cuba, in the meantime, will still be faced with the problems of being a small power dependent on a powerful ally—unless, through great effort, it manages to follow the course we have called "option three." The Cuban people can expect a slow but steady improvement in their economy; otherwise internal controls will remain in effect. But whatever the course of U.S.-Cuban relations in the next decade, there will be far more developments, possibly even dramatic ones, than we have seen in the last ten years.

Cover and book design: Pat Taylor